Philosophy of Architecture

建筑哲学

Philosophy
of Architecture

Christian Illies and Nicholas Ray
Chinese translation by Lina Tao

Liverpool University Press

Architecture and Philosophy is a rapidly growing subject and this introductory publication only covers the rough outilines of it. Numerous contributions have been made to the intersection of these two disciplines in the last fifty years, particularly by cultural historians, sociologists, anthropologists and geographers. We have confined ourselves for the most part to those debates that sit within the Western analytical tradition.

A shorter version of this book originally appeared as a chapter in a larger handbook: Christian Illies and Nicholas Ray, "Philosophy of Architecture", in *Philosophy of Technology and Engineering Sciences*, pp. 1199-1256, Elsevier, Burlington MA, Oxford & Amsterdam, 2009 (ISBN-13: 978-0-444-51667-1; ISBN-10: 0-444-51667-0). The generous support of CRASSH (the Centre for Research in the Arts, Social Sciences and Humanities) at the University of Cambridge, and of Delft and Eindhoven Universities of Technology, originally made our collaborative article possible.

Professor Kenneth Frampton suggested the chapter be turned into a book and with the assistance of Dr. Ranald Lawrence an expanded version was published by Cambridge Architectural Press in 2014 (ISBN 978-0-9930530-0-9).

Professor Stephanie Hemelryk Donald proposed a translation into Chinese and this has been undertaken by Lina Tao. Pingping Dou, Andong Lu and Yun Wu assisted with proof-reading.

Publication by Liverpool University Press was suggested and edited by Dr. Marco Iuliano. We are grateful to him and to Professor Pierre-Alain Croset for making this book possible.

Book layout by Luciano Striani

Cover image
Louis I. Kahn, *Parthenon*, 1951
Pastel on paper
© Sue Ann Kahn / Art Resource NY

Printed and bound by CPI Group (UK) Ltd, Croydon CR0 4YY
ISBN 9781786941695

contents
目录

Introduction

Two roles of a philosophy of architecture

This book considers the relationship between Western philosophy and architecture. We discuss philosophy's contribution to architecture and the way in which we can reflect philosophically about architecture, that is to say principally about individual buildings rather than cities.[1]

This double role of philosophy is unusual in the field of Technology and Engineering Sciences: a philosophical investigation would more often look critically at the process of gaining new knowledge or designing and producing something, or it would try to understand or evaluate types of artefacts (for example computers). In contrast, the practice of architecture is already deeply involved in and shaped by philosophical reflection and ideas. Architecture is guided by architectural theory, an ongoing discourse that bridges between philosophy and the practical discipline. Thus when philosophy looks at architectural artefacts or production, it investigates something that is *itself* partly philosophical, at least in the widest sense of the word.

Why architecture needs theory

That architectural practice is closely related to theory has been acknowledged for a long time. The Roman architect Vitruvius (ca. 80/70 - 25 BC), whose writing has exerted an unequalled influence on European architecture, at least since the Renaissance, argued for an inseparable link between the two:

> Architecture is a science arising out of many other sciences, and adorned with much and varied learning; by the help of which a judgment is formed of those works which are the result of other arts. Practice and theory are its parents. Practice is the frequent and continued contemplation of the mode of executing any given work, or of the mere operation of the hands, for the conversion of the material in the best and readiest way. Theory is the result of that reasoning which demonstrates and explains that the material wrought has been so converted as to answer the end proposed. Wherefore the mere practical architect is not able to assign sufficient reasons for the forms he adopts; and the theoretic architect also fails, obviously grasping the shadow instead of the real (*umbram non rem persecuti videntur*). He who is theoretic as well as practical, is therefore doubly armed; able not only to prove the propriety of his design, but equally so to carry it into execution. [Vitruvius, 2001, Chapter 1,1 - 1,2]

引言

建筑哲学的两种角色

本书探讨了西方哲学与建筑的关系。我们在此讨论了哲学对建筑的贡献，以及我们应该如何从哲学的角度去反思建筑。这里所说的建筑主要指单个建筑，而非城市。[1]

在技术工程科学领域，哲学的这种双重角色并不常见：这一领域的哲学研究通常是批判性地审视获取新知识或设计生产某事物的过程，抑或是试图理解或评估人工制品（例如电脑）。相比之下，建筑实践已经深刻参与到哲学思考与理念之中，并受到哲学思考与理念的支配。

建筑理论作为一个持续发展的话语体系，充当了哲学与建筑之间的桥，为建筑这门实践学科提供指导。所以，当我们以哲学视角审视建筑作品或产物时，所审视的事物本身就带有一定的哲学性，至少从哲学一词最广泛的语义上来说是这样的。

为什么建筑需要理论

建筑实践与理论紧密相关，这是长期以来公认的观点。罗马建筑学家维特鲁威（公元前约80/70-25）的著作曾对欧洲建筑——至少是文艺复兴以来的欧洲建筑——产生了无与伦比的影响。他认为建筑实践与理论之间存在着不可分割的联系：

建筑学是从诸多其他科学中衍生出来的一门科学，涉及各种各样的知识。建筑学有助于评判其他艺术门类的成果作品。实践和理论是建筑学之母。实践是为了以最佳、最简便的方式使用原材料，对执行任何给定工作的模式或者仅仅是双手的操作，进行频繁而持续的思考。而理论是推理过程的结果，这一推理过程证明并解释了如何使用原材料达到所计划的结果。因此，实用派的建筑师无法为他采取的形式提供充分的理由；而理论派的建筑师也同样不行，因为他们抓住的是影子，而非实相（*umbram non rem persecuti videntur*）。经过实用和理论双重武装的建筑师不仅能够证明其设计的适宜性，也能够同样地将该设计真正实施。（维特鲁威，2001，1.1-1.2章）

Vitruvius suggests that one of the characteristics of architecture is the role that theory plays for architects: they should be knowledgeable in many sciences and reflect upon what they do. Amongst other disciplines, Vitruvius wants the architect to be "acquainted with history, informed on the principles of natural and moral philosophy, somewhat of a musician, not ignorant of the sciences both of law and physics" [Vitruvius, 2001, Chapter 1.3]. And Vitruvius seems to suggest that these qualities are also present in the building: only if theory has guided the architect in the designing and building process, will the product be proper architecture.

Vitruvius' concept of "theory" is not identical to current understanding, of course, nor would such an emphasis on theory be unquestioned today.[2] Some have suggested that architecture could be a natural product of meeting society's needs, pointing to widely-admired "vernacular" buildings, and to the apparently inevitable way in which certain great buildings evolved within a tradition.[3] But in a self-conscious society with its complex demands it is unlikely that building can be such a natural activity (see, for example, [Rapoport, 1969]). Others warn against overburdening buildings with inappropriate social theories, when the criteria for judgement should be aesthetic (see, for example, [Scruton, 2000]). The Swiss architect Le Corbusier (1887-1965), who is often cited as an architect fixated by technology ("The house is a machine for living in" [Le Corbusier, 1946, p.89, p. 112], a statement frequently quoted out of context) believed that architecture is distinguished from buildings, or other engineered artefacts, not by theory's contribution but by the fact that it moves us *emotionally*:

> Finally, it will be a delight to talk of ARCHITECTURE after so many grain-stores, workshops, machines and skyscrapers. ARCHITECTURE is a thing of art, phenomenon of the emotions, lying outside questions of construction and beyond them. The purpose of construction is to HOLD THINGS TOGETHER; of architecture TO MOVE US. [Le Corbusier, 1946, p. 23][4]

But all these cases do not show that there can be architecture without some, possibly implicit theory. Le Corbusier's claim, for example, also implies a philosophical position – one that distinguishes "architecture" as having some special qualities that can move us emotionally, and involving some special skills that architects, as opposed to mere builders, would possess. There are strong reasons for thinking that architectural practice *necessarily* entails a theoretical position even if it is explicitly denied – at least if it is the result of conscious decisions.

Whereas there may be one or few *right* (in the sense of most efficient or functional) answer(s) to an engineering programme in other areas, once the parameters and goals have been correctly defined, there will always be more than one possible answer to an architectural problem. Thus architecture demands that conscious decisions are made between different forms and ideas – and therefore questions of judgement and interpretation are intrinsic to the discipline. Further, architecture is nearly always embedded in a culture, its ideas and ideals, its language of forms and its tradition, even if it is critical

维特鲁威认为，建筑的特点之一就在于理论对于建筑师们的重要性：他们应广泛涉猎诸多学科领域，并反思自己的工作。维特鲁威希望建筑师们能 "精研历史，了解自然与道德哲学的法则，熟悉音律，对法律和医学也略通一二。"（维特鲁威，2001，1.3章）。在维特鲁威看来，这些特质在建筑物中也有所体现：建筑师只有在设计和建造过程中得到理论的指引，才能创造出真正美好的建筑。

当然，维特鲁威关于"理论"的概念与当今的理解有所不同，他如此强调理论的重要性，如今也受到了一些质疑。[2] 有些人认为，建筑可以是为满足社会需求而出现的自然的产物，例如广受赞誉的"民间风格"建筑，还有一些伟大的建筑在沿袭传统时做出了非常必要的改进。[3] 但是，在一个充满自我意识、有着复杂需求的社会，建筑不太可能是一种自然而然的行为（可参考[拉普普特，1969]）。另一些人则告诫说，我们不应让建筑承载过多不合时宜的社会理论，对建筑的评判标准本应是美学（可参考[斯克鲁顿，2002]）。瑞士建筑学家勒•柯布西耶（1887-1965）作为一位技术派建筑学家，其观点常常被人们援引（"房屋是供居住的机器"[勒•柯布西耶，1946，89页，112页]，这一表述经常被人们断章取义地引用）。他认为，建筑与房屋或其他工程制品的区别，不仅是因为理论，而且是因为建筑能够在情感上打动我们：

> 在谈了这么多粮仓、车间、机器和摩天大楼之后，终于能愉悦地聊一聊建筑了。建筑是一门艺术，是情感的彰显，它与建造迥异，并且超越了建造。建造的目的是把材料拼装起来，而建筑的目的是让我们感动。[勒•柯布西耶，1946，p. 23][4]

但是这些例子都无法证明有的建筑不需要理论，理论可能是隐含在其中的。例如，勒•柯布西耶的观点同样指向了哲学立场——建筑具备某些能从情感上打动我们的特质，建筑学家们需要具备一些特殊的有别于建筑工人的技能。有充分的理由认为，建筑实践必然需要一个理论立场，即使该立场被明确否认，至少也是理智决定的结果。

针对其他领域的工程项目可能会有一个或几个正确的（即最有效或最实用的）答案，然而关于一个建筑问题，一旦正确设定了相关参数和目标，总会有不止一个的可行性方案。因此，建筑需要人们在不同的形式和思想之间做出清醒的决定，因而如何评判与解读是这一学科的固有问题。此外，建筑总是植根于某种文化、某种文化观念和理念、语言形式和文化传统，哪怕建筑对该文化

about it. The practical answers architecture gives to a problem (and the very formulation of the problem) will have to reflect this context. And reflection on a cultural context and on one's embeddedness *is* theory.[5] Thus as long as architecture is conscious, it will be accompanied by architectural theory – including theories about the exclusion of architectural theory, such as the romantic longings for a pre-theoretical vernacular way of building. As a public activity that stands at the heart of cultural life, architecture has also to address *fundamental* issues like questions of right and wrong in ethical matters, problems of the good life, or about meaning and its expression. It is here that architectural theory meets philosophical reflection, and all of its areas may be involved: logic, epistemology, ethics, aesthetics, philosophical anthropology and metaphysics, to name just the most important.

How philosophical theories intersect with architecture – some examples

Before outlining some of the philosophical themes that are relevant for the production and the appreciation of architecture, here are several examples that reveal how deeply architecture is intertwined with philosophical questions.

There are, for instance, ethical issues that begin even before the planning or design of a building: Architects must decide for whom they build at all: Rem Koolhaas (of OMA, the Office of Metropolitan Architecture) is the architect of the *Educatorium* of the University of Utrecht – certainly a worthy cause. But what about him accepting the commission to build the new headquarters for the Central Chinese Television (CCTV) Station, a €600m project in Beijing? Arguably, China's national TV station has played a supportive role within a regime that has a long record of human rights violation, and it has been suggested that architects should refuse to associate themselves with such a commission.[6] Certainly, whether architects choose to accept a request will often depend on the personal position that they hold. The Finnish architect Alvar Aalto, who regarded himself as something of an anarchist politically, built simultaneously for his wealthy Swedish-speaking patrons the Gullichsens and for the Finnish communist party – it is implied that architecture thereby in some way transcends the conditions of patronage to provide a good in itself.[7]

Ethical problems in architecture have at certain periods been more closely allied to architectural form and the problem of style. The problem only emerges when there are major choices to be made, so it was as a response to nineteenth-century eclecticism that A. W. N. Pugin (1812-1852) mounted a campaign to judge architecture on moral grounds [Pugin, 1843]. He argued that Gothic architecture was more "truthful" and "honest" in expressing the structure of a building, in employing materials in a way that was appropriate for the climate of northern Europe, and in its symbolisation of a Christian society. Such arguments are taken up by the influential critic John Ruskin (1819-1900), and appear in the twentieth century (but with different terminology and justifying a different set of forms) to support the claim that International Modernism, by purging itself of all superfluous embellishment, was the only honest way of building in a modern

持批判的态度。建筑对某一问题（以及该问题的形成过程）所给出的实际答案，将必然反映出它所处的环境。而对于文化环境的反思、对建筑植根性的反思便是理论。[5] 因此，只要建筑是理性的，它必然伴随着建筑理论，包括排斥建筑理论的种种理论，例如对某种先于理论的民间建造风格的罗曼蒂克式的憧憬。作为一种处于文化生活核心的公共活动，建筑同样需要解决一些重大问题，例如伦理中对与错的问题，美好生活的问题，或者关于意义以及意义表达的问题。正是在这里，建筑理论与哲学反思相遇，并可能涉及所有哲学领域：逻辑、认知论、伦理学、美学、哲学人类学以及形而上学，在此仅罗列了一些最重要的哲学领域。

哲学理论与建筑如何互相影响——一些案例

在罗列与建筑创作及鉴赏有关的几个哲学主题之前，以下几个案例展示了建筑是如何与哲学问题紧密交织在一起的。

举例来说，在开始规划或设计一幢建筑物之前就存在伦理的问题：建筑师必须确定他的客户到底是谁：雷姆·库哈斯（大都会建筑事务所的建筑师）设计建筑了乌特勒支大学教育馆，这显然是一项崇高的事业。但他接受委托设计建造中国中央电视台位于北京的、耗资约6亿欧元的新大楼，我们又该如何看待呢？可以说，中国的政治体制下存在着西方价值观无法接受的人权纪录，而中国国家电视台在这一体制里扮演了支持者的角色，因此有人认为建筑师们理应拒绝参与这种委托项目。[6] 当然，建筑家们是否选择接受邀约往往取决于他们个人所持的立场。芬兰建筑师阿尔瓦·阿尔托把自己看作某种意义上的无政府主义者，他曾同时为富有的瑞典客户古里奇森家族和芬兰共产党提供建筑设计——这说明建筑因此在某种意义上超越了出资者的范畴，而提供一种内在的善。[7]

在某些时期，建筑的伦理问题与建筑的形式和风格问题更为紧密相关。只有在需要作出重大决定时，这一问题才会出现，是对19世纪折衷主义的一种回应。折衷主义是普金（1812-1852）发起的一场以道德标准评判建筑的运动（普金，1843）。他认为哥特式建筑在表现建筑物结构、以适应北欧气候的方式使用建筑材料以及表征基督教社会等方面更为"坦诚"和"真实"。这种观点后来被富有影响力的评论家约翰·拉斯金（1819-1900）所引用，并在20世纪时再次涌现（但使用了不同的术语，用以支持另一套建筑形式）以支持下述论点，即：在清除一切华而不实的装饰后，国际现代主义是现代世界里唯一诚实的建造方式。

world. Critics have called this "the ethical fallacy", arguing that there is confusion here between moral and aesthetic questions.[8]

It is clear that developments of science affect the creation of new forms of architecture, though to what extent remains the focus for debate in every period. In medieval times, structural understanding was conditioned by the use of geometry, *ad quadratum* and *ad triangulatum*, which was both convenient, and carried iconological significance. By the Renaissance, however, Bramante's report on the vaulting of the crossing of the cathedral of Milan could treat the issue of statics foremost, whilst also considering issues of stylistic continuity. It is only in the seventeenth century that we encounter calculation of trusses beginning to determine the architectural form of roofs – it is no accident that the architect Christopher Wren was a member of the Royal Society, the pre-eminent scientific institute of its time. Yet the background to the possibility of this change is metaphysical and brought about by the new understanding of humans and the cosmos in the period of the Renaissance, which Jacob Burkhardt famously described as the "rise of the individual" in *The Civilization of the Renaissance in Italy* (1860). Following philosophers like Pico della Mirandola, the central tenet of the new anthropology reads: God has made humans as the masters of a world, a world that is intelligible and well-ordered and guided by natural laws. This contrasted with the medieval view which had emphasized the dependency of humans on God for their unique abilities. The new worldview found an expression in art's return to antiquity (and was also nurtured by what scholars and artists found there). In architecture, the rediscovery and use of anthropomorphic, classical members with the fully developed architrave show the new pride of being humans, thereby making the form of the human body the supportive element of edifices. Also the understanding of nature as an ordered cosmos is mirrored in architectural changes, like the Renaissance ideal of geometrical urban structures with spatial centralisation. A programmatic manifestation of the new spirit is the design of the ideal city "Sforzinda" by Filarete (1400-1469), which he planned for the Italian despot Ludovico Sforza of Milan. It is star-shaped, highly centralized, and streets and squares are defined by buildings which consist of the same stereometric units.

For Renaissance artists, architecture is meant to follow an understanding of man and nature, but we might ask from our current situation *which* understanding it should use as its starting point, and whether it is an ideal at all to build in harmony with a certain anthropology or cosmology. In an architectural debate between Christopher Alexander (born 1936) and Peter Eisenman (born 1932), Eisenman pleads for building in disharmonious, incongruent ways: "Alternative views of the world might suggest that it is not wholeness that will evoke our truest feelings and that it is precisely the wholeness of the anthropocentric world that it might be the presence of absence, that is, the nonwhole, the fragment which might produce a condition that would more closely approximate our innate feelings today."[9]

We might also ask if there is something "more" to (good) architecture – something that cannot be grasped by theory or measured precisely? In his books Christopher Alexander speaks about the "life" that good buildings should have and that architects

评论家们称之为"伦理谬论",认为这种说法混淆了道德与美学问题。[8]

科学的发展显然影响了建筑新形式的创造,只是影响程度有多大,一直是各时期争论的焦点。在中世纪,对结构的理解取决于对几何图形的运用,正方形和三角形既实用,又具有图像学意义。但是到文艺复兴时期,布拉曼特对米兰大教堂中央穹顶的报告可以说把对静态学问题的研究推向了极致,同时考虑到了风格连贯性的问题。到17世纪,人们才开始计算桁架以确定屋顶的建筑形式——建筑学家克里斯托弗·列恩同时是当时最卓越的科学机构皇家学会的成员,此事绝非偶然。然而,这一变革的背景却是形而上的,是由文艺复兴时期对人类和宇宙的新认知所引起的,雅各布·布克哈特在《意大利文艺复兴时期的文化》(1860)一书中称之为"个人的崛起"。遵循哲学家皮科·德拉·米兰多拉等人的观点,新兴人类学的核心原则是:上帝让人类做世界的主人,而这世界明白易懂,井然有序,由自然法则引导。这与中世纪的观点形成了对比,后者强调人类对自身独特能力的依赖。这种新的世界观通过艺术对古典的回归找到了一种表现形式(而且学者和艺术家们对古典的发掘也滋养了这种新的世界观)。在建筑学中,对带有成熟额枋的人格化经典构件的重新发现和运用,显示了作为人类的新骄傲,从而使得人体样式成为大型建筑物的支持性元素。另外,把自然看作是有序的宇宙这一认知也反映在建筑的演变当中,例如文艺复兴时期对空间集中的几何型城市构造的憧憬。体现这一新思想的范例是菲拉雷特(1400-1469)为意大利统治者、米兰公爵卢多维科· 斯福尔扎设计的理想城市"斯福钦达"。这个星形城市高度集中,街道和广场的边界是由相同的立体单元所构成的建筑物划定的。

对于文艺复兴时期的艺术家们而言,建筑应当符合对人与自然的认知,但我们结合当今的形势可能要问,应该采用哪种认知作为建筑的出发点,而且让建筑与某种人类学或宇宙学保持和谐一致是否真的只是一种理想。在克利斯托弗·亚历山大(生于1936年)和彼得·艾森曼(生于1932年)进行的建筑学争论中,艾森曼为不协调、不和谐的建筑方式进行辩护:"非传统的世界观或许说明,并不是整体性激发了我们最真实的感情,恰恰是在以人类为中心的世界整体性当中缺位的存在,即非整体性、碎片化,所创造的环境更加接近我们当下的内在感受。"[9]

或许我们还要问(好的)建筑是否蕴含着"更多"的东西,某些不能被理论捕捉或精确测量的东西?克利斯托弗·亚历山大在其著作中谈到了好的建筑应该是有"生命"的,当建筑师们

can create when they have a feeling for it [Alexander, 2002]; others have talked about the generation of "place" rather than "space", or of a location that allows us to "dwell". "The nature of building is letting dwell", as the German philosopher Martin Heidegger (1889-1976) put it; he linked dwelling to a form of human existence that is in harmony with "Being". He observed such harmony in the "dwelling" of farmers in the Black Forest and that is why their buildings are good buildings: "Only if we are capable of dwelling, only then can we build" [Heidegger, 1951, p. 362].

Short overview

In what follows, we will examine the ways in which philosophy intersects with architecture; in particular we will look at the way philosophy has been relevant for the reflection upon and for the production of architecture.

In the next section, we investigate how philosophical ideas have shaped architecture and its theory. We focus on different, often oppositional approaches: Plato's philosophy of ideal forms and its role for Renaissance architecture is our first case, followed by an analysis of the ideas that have given birth to architectural Historicism in the 19th century. Heidegger and his importance for critical regionalism and new urbanism is discussed and, finally, Postmodernism and other post-metaphysical philosophies and their importance for architecture.

In the third section we investigate ways in which architecture can be looked at ethically. There are several, rather different ways that can be distinguished – and given that some of them seem of high importance for our life as human beings, we find it surprising that philosophers of ethics have given so little attention to architecture.

We move on to Aesthetics in the fourth section, asking how do different aesthetic theories shape architecture and our understanding of it? Among the fundamental questions raised in this section are: what are the key categories for an appreciation of architecture? And how is the relationship between buildings as functional artefacts and aesthetic objects to be understood?

Finally, in the fifth section, we shift the focus towards the activity of design: the work of three twentieth and twenty-first century designers (Kahn, Koolhaas, and Aalto) is examined in more detail. We analyse how the production of architecture, as well as its reception, may indicate a philosophical stance. Sometimes this may be explicit, since the architects are clearly claiming a position.[10] Sometimes the architects' intentions are not stated, or if they are they seem to be negated by the experience of the work itself, and then critics and historians tend to interpret the artefacts in the light of the prevailing cultural context.

The book ends with a short reflection on what it has achieved, and suggests some directions for the future of philosophy of architecture.

对这种生命有感受时，就能够创造它（亚历山大，2002）；其他人曾谈到"住所"而非"空间"的生成，或者说是容纳我们"栖居"的某个地方的产生。如同德国哲学家马丁·海德格尔（1889-1976）说的那样："建筑的本质是供人居住的"；他把栖居看作是人类的一种生活方式，这种生活方式是与存在和谐一致的。他在黑森林农庄里农民们的"住所"那里看到了这种和谐，这就是为什么他们的建筑是好的建筑："只有当我们能够栖居时，我们才能够建造"（海德格尔，1951，362页）。

章节概述

在下文中，我们将探讨哲学与建筑发生关联的各种方式；我们尤其关注哲学对于建筑反思和建筑创造的相关性。

在下一章节，我们将探讨哲学思想是如何塑造建筑及建筑理论的。我们重点关注不同的、甚至常常是彼此对立的各种方式：我们首先关注的是柏拉图关于理想形式的哲学以及它在文艺复兴建筑当中的角色，然后分析孕育19世纪建筑历史主义的各种思想。我们还分析了海德格尔和他对批判性地域主义和新城市主义的重大影响，最后探讨后现代主义和其他后形而上学等哲学思想，以及它们对建筑的重要性。

在第三章节我们将探讨以伦理看待建筑的若干方式。这里有几种截然不同的、彼此可以区分开来的方式，其中一些方式对我们人类的生活极为重要，但我们却发现伦理哲学家们极少关注建筑，这令我们感到很诧异。

接下来在第四章节里我们关注的是美学，所研究的问题是，不同的美学理论如何影响了建筑以及我们对建筑的理解？这一章所提出的若干基本问题包括：建筑鉴赏有几个重要类别？建筑物作为功能性人工产物和需要被理解的美学对象之间存在怎样的关系？

最后，在第五章节，我们将关注点转向设计活动，更加细致地考察了三位二十世纪和二十一世纪的设计师的作品（康、库哈斯和阿尔托）。我们分析了建筑的创作过程及其反响情况是如何传递出哲学立场的。有些情况下，这种立场是明确的，因为建筑师们清楚地表明了其立场。[10] 但有时建筑师们并未说明其意图，或者对作品本身的体验否定了建筑师的意图，然后评论家们和历史学家又倾向于依据当时的文化背景对建筑作品进行解读。

在结尾处，我们对本书的主要结论做了简要总结，并对建筑哲学未来的方向提出了一些建议。

Philosophical ideas and worldviews

Ideas and clichés

Architectural theory is nurtured by philosophical ideas; the concerns and questions that move people at a certain time as much as their visions and worldviews are mirrored in their buildings: Architecture provides functional and technical solutions but is also a practical answer to philosophical questions.

Yet to account for philosophy's role for architecture one faces a profound difficulty: Architects have often read philosophers in ways that scholars find very problematic. Because architectural debates are embedded in wider reflections of a culture, they are shaped as much by clichés as by ideas that are current at any time. Misunderstandings may also be influential. As an example, Spinoza, though his philosophy is in fact an extreme form of rationalism, became one of the cultural heroes of romanticism. A further complication stems from the often muddled use of concepts within architectural theory, that is neither congruent within the debate of the discipline, nor in harmony with philosophical usage. People simply mean very different things when they use words such as "function" or "deconstruction".[11]

We will therefore look at philosophers and philosophical ideas in the way that they were interpreted and utilized by architects, independent from whether their reading should be seen as a correct or even plausible interpretation. Let us first turn to Plato whose importance can hardly be overestimated: his vision of a world of ideas or forms behind or above empirical reality inspired architecture for centuries. Building became a quest for the manifestation of such Platonic ideals.

Plato's philosophy of ideal forms

Plato famously argued for the possibility of grasping "ideas" or "forms", that is a space- and time-less realm of subject-independent principles (or universals) that ultimately provide the structure and character of our world (or the particulars). Among the most important of these ideas are goodness and beauty, but there are also mathematical ideas (like geometric forms) and ideas of empirical objects (such as of a tree, a horse, or a house). For Plato, these ideas are more perfect and real than the empirical world, because they are the paradigmatic models of all that is. A famous example is the circle: all circles that we see or draw are necessarily imperfect to some degree, but they are circles by being approximations to the mathematical idea of a perfect circle. Without

哲学理念与世界观

思想与传统观念

  建筑理论受到了哲学思想的滋养；那些在某一特定时期触动人们并影响其见解和世界观的重大命题与问题，都会通过建筑物反映出来：建筑给出了功用性、技术性的解决方案，同时也是对哲学问题的实际回答。

  要解释哲学对建筑的影响并非易事：在学者们看来，建筑学家对哲学家的解读方式有很大的问题。由于建筑学的争论根植于对某种文化的更宽泛的反思，这些争论既受当下时代思想的影响，也同样受到传统观念的影响。误读可能也会产生很大的影响。举例来说，虽然斯宾诺莎的哲学实际上是理性主义的极端形式，但他却成为了浪漫主义的文化伟人之一。让问题更为复杂化的是建筑理论中对概念的混乱使用，既与建筑学科内的讨论不一致，也与哲学界的概念使用不一致。当人们使用"功能"或"解构"这类词语时，他们所指的却是完全不同的事物。[11]

  因此，我们要探讨的是建筑学家们对哲学家及其哲学思想的解读与使用方式，而不去考虑这样的解读是否正确或合理。我们首先来看柏拉图，其重要性无论怎样形容都不为过：他认为在经验现实之上或背后有一个思想与形式之邦，这成为千百年来建筑的灵感来源。建筑物成为了力图呈现柏拉图式理想的一种探索。

柏拉图关于理想形式的哲学

  关于捕捉"理念"或"形式"的可能性，柏拉图有着著名的论断，即一个超越了空间与时间的领域，以独立于主体之外的原理（或共相）最终为我们这个世界（或具相）提供了结构和特征。其中最重要的两种理念是善和美，但此外也有一些数学的理念（例如几何形式）和关于经验客体（例如一棵树、一匹马或一座房子）的理念。对柏拉图而言，这些理念比经验世界更为完美和真实，因为它们是一切万有的模型典范。一个著名的例子是圆：所有我们看到的或画出来的圆在某种程度上必然是不完美的，但它们近似于数学理念中那个完美的圆，因而称其为圆。离开了

17

having this idea, we would not regard these imperfect instantiations as circles. Plato refers to Socrates' seemingly paradoxical remark that he who sees merely with his eyes is blind. For Plato, the invisible world is the most intelligible while the visible world is obscure and least knowable.

Plato's position is most famously captured in the Allegory of the Cave in his *Republic* [Plato, 1945, 7.514a ff]. Here Plato compares our situation with that of people who live in a dark cave and merely see the shadows of things that are projected by a fire at the wall of the cave; these shadows are the empirical world that we mistake for the true reality. Our task is to break through this ignorance – Plato talks about us being chained to chairs in front of the shadow-theatre-wall – and seeking to climb up to the true sunlight outside the cave, namely the ideas. Those who reach this light will have objective knowledge about how things really are.

Although Plato's discussions in the dialogues are often about epistemological issues, his epistemology was embedded in an ontology – and this position became more important for the architectural tradition. For Plato, it seems, only these forms truly exist while empirical things are of a secondary order. Plato was, with regard to *all* reality, including mathematics, aesthetics and ethics, an "Idealist Objectivist", because forms, that is the (true) objective reality, were ultimately seen as non-material.

For Plato, these forms also have a normative (or ethical) side to them. By being models for empirical reality, they also show us how things ideally should be. His analysis of the craftsperson illustrates this point. Carpenters who construct a house need to know the idea of a house. That gives them the direction towards the perfect house: it will tell them how a house *ought* to be built, and how the materials ought to be used and arranged. To update the analogy: by knowing the idea, they know the stresses and the strains and, most importantly, the right proportions. The idea of the house is a kind of blueprint to follow, and only if we approximate it will we have a good house (or any house at all, since a bad house will collapse). Ideas tell us not only what there is, but also what we should strive to realize. This ideal is captured by Plato's term "imitation" (*mimesis*) that became crucial in the aesthetic theory of his pupil Aristotle: If the ideas or forms are superior and paradigmatic, artworks should try to imitate these ideals – sometimes also called the "essence" or "nature" of things. This principle became most influential, though its concretisation differed widely due to varying understanding of what these ideas or forms are and what it means to imitate them.[12]

The influence on architecture of Platonism (and Neo-platonism, the views of followers of Plato from the third century BC onwards, and evident also in the middle ages) can be seen most clearly in the Renaissance. This was the time when Plato's work was rediscovered, and it was incorporated into a new interpretation of Christianity. Leon Battista Alberti (1404-1472) wrote an influential book on architecture, *De re aedificatoria*, modelled on Vitruvius' ten books, but with a much more clearly argued thesis [Alberti, 1988].[13] In relation to geometry, he claimed that pure forms, like the circle and the square, were closest to the divine; they should therefore be reserved for religious buildings, while less important buildings, such as houses, could

这个理念，我们就不会把这些不完美的具象看作是圆。柏拉图引用了苏格拉底一个看似矛盾的观点，即一个只用眼睛去看的人是盲的。对柏拉图来说，那个不可见的世界是最可知的，而可见的世界却是模糊的、最不可知的。

关于柏拉图的立场，最著名的例子是他在《理想国》里提出的洞穴寓言[柏拉图，1945，7.514a ff]。在书中柏拉图把我们的处境比作居住在黑暗洞穴里的人们，他们只能看到事物被火光投射在洞穴墙上的影子；这些影子就是被我们错认做真实的经验世界。我们的任务是打破这种无知——柏拉图把我们看作是被绑在椅子上、面对着投影墙的囚徒，需要攀爬到洞穴外才能看到真正的阳光，即理念。那些接触到这光的人将获得关于事物真相的客观知识。

虽然柏拉图在对话集里所讨论的往往是认识论的问题，其认识论却是植根于本体论的——这一立场对建筑传统尤为重要。对柏拉图而言，似乎只有这些形式是真实存在的，而可经验的事物处于次要位置。关于万有的真相，包括数学、美学和伦理学，柏拉图可以说是一位"理想主义的客观主义者"，因为他认为形式，即（真实的）客观存在，从根本上说是非物质的。

对柏拉图来说，这些形式也有规范性（或伦理性）的一面。作为经验事实之模板，这些形式向我们展示了事物的理想状态应该是什么样的。他通过对木匠的分析阐释了这一点。一个造房子的木匠需要了解房子的理念。这种理念将指导他建造一栋完美的房子；它会告诉他应该如何筑造一栋房子以及如何使用和安排材料。把这个比喻更进一步：木匠在了解理念之后，就掌握了压力和拉力，更重要的是适当的比例。房子的理念就像是一个需要遵循的蓝本，只有当我们不断向它靠近时才能造出好的房子（或者说造出任何房子，因为坏房子终会倒塌）。这理念不仅告诉我们那里有什么，也告诉我们应该努力实现什么。柏拉图用术语"模仿"（mimesis）传达了这一理想，这个术语对于他的学生亚里士多德的美学理论至关重要：如果说理念或形式是更高级的、典范式的，那么艺术作品应该尽可能去模仿这些理想的事物——有时也被称作事物的"实质"或"本质"。虽然对理念或形式是什么、模仿它们意味着什么有着不同的理解，对该原则的具体实践也千差万别，但不可否认这一原则的影响极为深远。[12]

柏拉图主义（以及新柏拉图主义，即公元前三世纪以来、在中世纪也有所彰显的柏拉图追随者们的观点）对建筑的影响在文艺复兴时期展露无遗。在这一时期柏拉图的作品被重新发现，并被融入到对基督教的新的解读当中。莱昂·巴蒂斯塔·阿尔伯蒂（1404-1472）著有一本影响深远的建筑学著作《论建筑》，仿照维特鲁威《建筑十书》的样式，但其论点论述要清楚得多（阿尔伯蒂，1988）。[13] 关于几何学，他声称圆和方等等这种纯正的形式最接近神性；所以它们应该为宗教建筑所专用，而不那么重要的建筑物，譬如普通房屋，可以

have a more casual and pragmatic form. Thus geometry serves to reinforce our sense of propriety. The claim of Le Corbusier, explaining the affect that architecture (as opposed to mere building) can have on people, and arguing that "pure forms are beautiful forms", not only suggests that decoration is redundant in the twentieth century but echoes Alberti's prescriptions (albeit aesthetically rather than in their religious sense), and eventually a platonic view that actual artefacts aspire to an ideal form.[14] This eschewal of decoration was a particularly twentieth-century phenomenon, however: for Alberti decoration was an important aspect of *decor* or "appropriateness". In Book 6, chapter 2, he makes a clear distinction between ornament, which consists of the correct use of the classical orders in their proper proportions, and beauty, which he famously defined as "that reasoned harmony of all the parts within a body, so that nothing may be added, taken away, or altered, but for the worse":

> Ornament may be defined as a form of auxiliary light and complement to beauty. From this follows, I believe, that beauty is some inherent property, to be found suffused all through the body of that which may be called beautiful; whereas ornament, rather than being inherent, has the character of something attached or additional.

Beauty is thus the essential idea, whereas ornament is an embellishment. Alberti returns to these distinctions in Book 9. But when we make judgements on beauty, he argues, we do not merely follow our fancies, because reasoning is involved. There are three components: "number, what we might call outline, and position". Composition is the art of bringing these components together, and when they are perfectly harmonious they represent what Alberti called *concinnitas*.

Alberti also makes practical suggestions on how to achieve the "reasoned harmony of all the parts", and some have pointed to how his own buildings illustrate them.[15] In Book 7, chapter 15, he states that "for arched colonnades quadrangular columns are required". This is not only for technical reasons (because these can be overcome), but also because Alberti understands an arched opening to be a break in a wall, a kind of curved beam. It is therefore logical that its supports should be pieces of wall, that is to say quadrangular, whereas the applied ornament of a pediment would use engaged columns. Alberti's own *Tempio Malatestiano*, the transformation of the 13th century San Francesco at Rimini for Sigismondo Malatesta, constructed from 1450 but never completed, illustrates the theory. The powerful blank arcade at the side has massive piers, and turns around to the west front of the church; the entablature above is supported by elegant Corinthian halfcolumns. The well-proportioned arched wall architecture, obeying the principle of *concinnitas*, could be said to represent beauty, and the applied columns are the appropriate ornament. Both the proportioning of the parts and the application of decoration serve to ennoble the building and transform it into a *tempio* (with the neo-platonic associations that suggests), which is suitable to act as a mausoleum for the patron and his wife.

采用一种更为随意和实用的形式。因此，几何学有助于增强我们的规范意识。勒·柯布西耶阐述了建筑（不同于单纯的筑造物）可能对人产生的影响，并提出"纯正的形式是美的形式"，他的这一观点认为装饰在二十世纪是多余的，而且呼应了阿尔伯蒂的训示（尽管是从美学的而非宗教的角度），也最终呼应了柏拉图式的观点，即真正的人工作品是对理想形式的追求。[14] 然而，这种对装饰的规避是二十世纪所特有的现象：对阿尔伯蒂来说，装饰是布置或"适合性"的一个重要方面。在第六书第二章里，他对装饰和美作了清晰的区分，前者是对经典秩序依照其恰当的比例而做出的正确使用，而针对后者他也给出了著名的定义，即"美是一个物体内部所有部分之间的理性的和谐，增之一分则多，减之一分则少，任何一点点改变都只会让它变得糟糕"：

> 装饰可以被看做是对美的一种辅助和补充形式。由此延伸开来，我的观点是，美是一种内在的属性，可以在一个被称为美的物体中处处得到体现；但是装饰并不是内在的，而是某种添加的或额外的事物特性。

因此，美是最核心的理念，而装饰则是一种修饰。阿尔伯蒂在第九书中重申了两者的区别。不过他认为，当我们评判美时，我们不只是遵循我们的爱好，也涉及到推理论证。其中有三个组成部分："数字，所谓的轮廓线，以及位置"。创作是把这些部分融合为一体的艺术，当它们达到完美的和谐时，所呈现的就是阿尔伯蒂所说的"均整和谐"。

至于如何实现"各个部分的理性和谐"，阿尔伯蒂也给出了一些实际的建议，还有些人结合阿尔贝蒂本人的建筑，指出他的这些建议如何在其自身的建筑中得到了体现。[15] 在第七书第15章，阿尔伯蒂写道："拱形的石柱廊要用四边形柱"。这不仅是出于技术的原因（当然它能解决技术问题），也是因为阿尔伯蒂认为拱形洞是墙面的中断，是一种弯曲梁，因此从逻辑上说，它的支撑物应该是一部分墙面，也就是四边形，而三角形楣饰的外加装饰要用嵌墙柱。阿尔伯蒂所建的马拉泰斯塔庙宇证明了这一理论。受西吉斯蒙多·马拉泰斯塔所托，阿尔伯蒂对位于里米尼的13世纪圣弗朗切斯科教堂进行改造，从1450年起开始建造，但始终未能竣工。建筑侧面风格浑厚、无装饰的拱廊有着巨大的支座，并转向教堂的西侧正面。柱上楣构由优雅的科林斯式半柱支撑。这一比例良好的拱形墙建筑遵循了均整和谐的原则，可以说呈现了美，而那些外加的立柱是恰当的装饰。各部分的比例和对装饰的运用使建筑物变得尊贵，并将其改造成一座神殿（反映出了与新柏拉图主义的关联性），因此适宜作为资助人及其妻室的陵墓。

Historicism in philosophy and architecture

An architecture of association, rather than one derived from the authority of the ancients, appears for the first time in the mid eighteenth century. Its first manifestations are in garden buildings, and the influence is as much literary as architectural. By the middle to the end of the nineteenth century, all over Europe we find an eclectic Historicism. The style of the time involves the revival of numerous historical styles, beginning with a regained appreciation of the Gothic, but soon turning to other epochs. A dominant example of such a turning away from classicism was the new parliament building in London, by Barry and Pugin from 1840, at least in its decoration. Internationally, architects used architectural motifs from the antique or from the exotic east, such as India, China or Japan, often employing different styles to the facade and to interiors. We find (neo-) gothic cathedrals (everywhere), (neo-) baroque opera-houses (e.g. Paris), factories that looked like mosques (e.g. Dresden), or train stations with renaissance campaniles (e.g. Erfurt). Historicism is striking for its seemingly random combination of different stylistic elements from one or more epochs – when Leo von Klenze designed the *Königsplatz* as the new centre of Munich, he built a 1:1-replica of the *Propylaeum* (from the Athenian Acropolis) with two side-towers in an Egyptian style.

The term "Historicism", however, has different meanings. In his essay "Three kinds of Historicism", Alan Colquhoun mentions three dominant definitions [Colquhoun, 1985, p. 202]: firstly "the theory that all socio-cultural phenomena are historically determined", secondly "a concern for the institutions and traditions of the past", and finally "the use of historical forms". While the third definition covers the artistic (and architectural) style of the nineteenth century, the first definition refers to the philosophical ideas that have shaped this style – namely the idea that all historical phenomena have a unique or singular character because they are not expressions of timeless principles but determined by the situation and context.[16] People began to study different epochs and cultures in order to understand them in their own terms rather than searching for the allegedly universal principles behind them. The other side of this conception is to understand the world, or nature, as being in a state of permanent change – unstable rather than fixed or permanent.

In order to understand how philosophical and architectural Historicism are connected, we should look more closely at the philosophical ideas behind Historicism, at least as it was generally understood. The new approach seemed to be supported by Kant's critical epistemology, according to which we have no direct awareness of pure sense-data, but select and shape them; we apprehend sense-data only as unified and structured by *a priori* categories of the mind. Rather than being a passive receiver of information, about how the world is, the mind plays an active and creative role in the process of cognition. Consequently, all knowledge is seen as perspectival in character; it is not a discovery of the objective reality (let alone of the essence of, or ideas behind, reality) so much as a social or individual creation.

Historicism can also be seen to follow Hegel's analysis of history, and the discovery, by him and others, that the categories and ordering principles of the mind have

哲学和建筑中的历史主义

在十八世纪中叶首次出现了文化关联型建筑，不再依赖于古典权威。它最初体现在花园建筑中，其对文学的影响和对建筑的影响一样大。我们发现，19世纪中期至末期的整个欧洲出现了一种兼收并蓄的历史主义。这一时期有不计其数的历史风格重新流行，起初是人们对哥特式风格重拾兴趣，其后很快又转向其他时期的风格。背离古典主义的一个主要例证是由巴利和普金自1840年设计建造的伦敦新国会大厦，至少它的装饰反映了这一点。在国际上，建筑师们使用复古的装饰图案，或是来自印度、中国或日本等东方国家的装饰图案，通常对建筑物的外立面和内部采用不同的风格。我们看到（新）哥特式的大教堂（比比皆是），（新）巴洛克式的歌剧院（例如巴黎），酷似清真寺的工厂（例如德累斯顿），或是带有文艺复兴风格钟楼的火车站（例如爱尔福特）。历史主义的引人注目之处，在于它对一个或多个时期不同风格元素的看似随意的组合——利奥·冯·克伦泽在设计作为慕尼黑新中心的国王广场时，以1:1的比例复制了雅典卫城的山门，两个侧塔则采用了埃及风格。

但是，"历史主义"一词有着不同的含义。艾伦·科尔奎恩在他的文章《三种历史主义》里提到了三种主流定义（科尔奎恩，1985，202页）：第一种是"所有社会文化现象都是由历史决定的这一理论"，第二是"对以往的体制与传统的关注"，第三是"对历史形式的运用"。第三种定义涵盖了19世纪的艺术（和建筑）风格，而第一种定义则指出了形成这一风格的哲学理念，即所有的历史现象都有其独特的或单一的特征，因为它们并非永恒法则的体现，而是由形势与情境决定的。[16]人们着手研究不同的时代和文化，目的是为了理解这些时代和文化本身，而不是找寻其背后所谓的普遍性原则。这一概念的另一面是认识到世界或自然界处于持续变化的不稳定状态中，而非固定或永恒的。

为了理解哲学历史主义和建筑历史主义之间的关联，我们应该更深入地考察历史主义——至少要考察人们所普遍理解的那种历史主义——背后的哲学理念。这种更为自由的解读历史的态度似乎受到了康德的批判性认识论的支持，按照康德的观点，我们并不能直接察觉纯粹的感官材料，而是在挑选和塑造这些材料；我们在理解感官材料时，会按照思想中先天存在的范畴去统一和组织这些材料。关于对世界的理解，思想并不是在被动地接收信息，而是在认知过程中发挥着积极的、创造性的作用。结果就是，所有的知识可以说从特征上说是视角化的；它并不是对客观现实的发现（更不用说是事实背后的本质或理念了），而是社会或个人的创造。

历史主义也可以说遵循了黑格尔的历史分析，并延续了他和另外一些人的发现，即思想的范畴及其秩序规则

changed with the succession of cultures and epochs: the historicity of the human mind. When we look at the past, we find not one interpretation of the world but instead a variety of perspectives or worldviews. Thus Historiography should be about an "objective and exhaustive examination of facts" and the "attempt to penetrate the essential spirit of the country or period being studied" – that means to understand a time in its own terms [Colquhoun, 1985, p. 204]. Hegel, however, was still presupposing a (dialectic) teleology as an internal logic of the developments of the diverse cultures and epochs; later historicists have given up any such assumption, explaining changes in terms of the adjustment of individuals and groups to life under different historical and social conditions. This is accompanied by a rejection of any evaluation; no period is inferior or superior to another – "every age is next to God", as Leopold von Ranke famously said.

This philosophical position offers an explanation of the architectural historicist combination of different style elements: an artistic style was seen as an expression of a time, its culture and values, and no longer of eternal truth. As a result, no style was better than another; they all merely mirrored different cultures with their aesthetic ideals. Thus classicism was no longer privileged over other styles, instead styles became a matter of association or the architect chose the style that seemed suitable for particular purposes: a church might be Gothic, the style of medieval Christianity, whereas a library, to house classic texts from antiquity, could itself be classical. And King Ludwig I of Bavaria (1786-1868) wanted his capital Munich to be seen as a second Athens.

One of the more radical consequences of 19th century perspectivism is the claim that all truth is relative. Each epoch or culture, historicism claims, develops its own view of the world in its totality because of the different values, categories and presuppositions upon which its cognition is based. But if these categories are themselves essentially variable and arbitrary, then all claims to an objective grasp of reality (let alone absolute knowledge) are baseless in principle – each epoch and culture has its own truth. As Colquhoun writes, the new insight was that "each culture could adhere only to its own notion of the true and the false, through values that were immanent in particular social and institutional forms." [Colquhoun, 1985, p. 204] The position was developed comprehensively by Friedrich Nietzsche, for whom we literally make reality, and make our own truths. The only supratemporal, or "absolute" truth that might be found is this very insight, namely that no absolute truths about the nature of things are possible. The idea of the relativity of all knowledge and worldviews is characteristic of modernity: Nietzsche blamed his time for being unable or unwilling to accept this insight and draw the inevitable conclusions from it.

Nietzsche's critique of reason as the main tool for understanding and mastering reality has also had a profound influence. He famously made this point when he proposed the rehabilitation of the irrational ecstatic element in culture that he found exemplified in Dionysius, the god of intoxication. He contrasted Dionysian with Apollonian characteristics and saw both as sources of cultural production in Greek antiquity [Nietzsche, 1872]. Rational thought is Apollonian in character since it is structured and makes analytic distinctions; the Dionysian instinct, on the other hand, is characterized

会随着文化和时代的更迭而改变，也即人类思想的历史性。当我们回顾过去，我们会发现当时对世界的解读不止一种，而是有着多种多样的视角或世界观。所以，历史学应该是一种"对事实的客观而全面的考察"，是"试图洞悉所研究的国家或时期的根本精神"——这意味着去理解一个时代本身[科尔奎恩，1985，204页]。但是，黑格尔仍然预先假定了一种（辩证的）目的论作为多元文化和时代发展的内在逻辑；之后的历史学家们放弃了这种假设，他们把变化看做是人和群体在不同的历史和社会条件下为了生活所做出的调整。随之而来的是对各种评判的摒弃；没有一个时代比另一个时代更好或者更差，就像利奥波德·冯·兰克的名言说的那样，"每一个时代都是最独特的"。

这一哲学立场可以解释建筑历史主义对不同风格元素的组合：一种艺术风格被看做是对一个时代及其文化与价值观的表达，而不再是对终极真理的表达。因此，无论哪种风格都是最好的；所有的风格只不过反映了不同的文化及其审美理想。所以古典主义与其他风格相比不再是高高在上的，相反，风格只与人们的文化参照有关，或者说，建筑师根据特定的目的去选择相应的风格：一座教堂可能是哥特式的、中世纪基督教的风格；而一个容纳古老典籍的图书馆本身可能就是古典的风格。巴伐利亚国王路德维希一世（1786—1868）则希望把他的首府慕尼黑打造成第二个雅典。

19世纪的视角主义所带来的一个更为深远的影响是所有真理都是相对的这一论断。历史主义宣称，每一个时代或文化发展出了自成一体的世界观，因为其认知建立在不同的价值观、范畴和预设的基础上。但是，如果这些范畴本身实际上是易变的、武断的，那么所有客观掌握真相的论断从原则上来说就失去了根基（更不用说掌握绝对的知识了）——每一个时代和文化都有各自的真理。正如科尔奎恩所说，新的见解就是"借助于特定社会和组织形式传递的固有价值观，每一种文化都只能遵循其自身关于真与假的观念。"[科尔奎恩，1985，204页]弗里德里希·尼采全面发展了这一观点，他认为，我们可以说就是在创造现实，创造我们自己的真理。我们可能找到的唯一超越时间的，或者说"绝对"的真理就是这一观点，即不可能有关于事物本质的绝对真理。所有的知识和世界观都具有相对性，这一理念正是现代性的特征：尼采指责他所处的时代不能或不愿接受这个见解以及基于该见解所得出的结论——虽然这个结论是毋庸置疑的。

尼采对于理性作为了解和掌握现实的主要工具所做的批判同样有着深远的影响。他建议恢复文化当中的非理性、令人狂喜的元素，并以酒神狄俄尼索斯为例，同时提出了著名的理性批判的论点。他对比了酒神和阿波罗神的特征，把两者都看做是古希腊文化产生的源泉[尼采，1872]。理性思维是阿波罗神的特征，因为它是结构化的，能够进行分析辨别；与此相反的是，酒神的本能

by irrationality, violence and chaotic emotions, but also by creative enthusiasm and exuberance. Nietzsche points out that from Socrates onward the Apollonian had dominated Western culture and thought and demands that we rediscover the "dark" side of art – as exemplified by the *Gesamtkunstwerk* of Richard Wagner, who was hailed as a saviour by Nietzsche, at least for a short time. Nietzsche values art very highly not because it gives us access to a higher ideal world, but because, believing existence to be absurd, he thought art, uniquely, had the capacity to assist in rendering "the terror and horror of existence" bearable.[17] This, however, could only be achieved by a radically renewed art of an individual genius who opposes the taste of his time and bravely walks his own way. Nietzsche, although philosophically a historicist, attacked much of historicist culture.

Nietzsche influenced many architects (and artists) at the end of the nineteenth century and beyond, especially of the *Art Nouveau* movement. Henri van der Velde (1863-1957) refers directly to Nietzsche as a prime source of inspiration for his work. He followed his sharp critique of bourgeois culture and was inspired by Nietzsche's vision of renewing European culture through an art that, very much like a *Gesamtkunstwerk*, unites form and content, art and daily life, public and private identity. Van der Velde happily built the Nietzsche archive in Weimar (1902-03) and planned a Nietzsche-Stadion (1911-1913). In America, aspects of Nietzsche's writings inspired the prose of Louis Sullivan (1856-1924), whose *Autobiography of an Idea* and 1886 *Essay on Inspiration* owes as much to German romanticism as to the poetry of Walt Whitman.[18] It is particularly telling that he talks about himself in the third person: Louis is portrayed as a heroic figure who is destined to overcome the petty obstructions placed in his way in pursuit of his art. Another architect who consistently referred to himself in the third person was Le Corbusier – born Charles-Edouard Jeanneret-Gris: in 1920 he founded the magazine *L'Esprit Nouveau* with the painter Amédée Ozenfant and adopted his pseudonym. Le Corbusier's thinking is complex, influenced by his voluminous reading, but we know that at the impressionable age of twenty-two he visited Paris for the first time and devoured Renan's *Life of Christ* and Nietzsche's *Thus spake Zarathustra*. According to William Curtis, "this was a time of turmoil in which he wavered between certainty of his Olympian role and deep self-doubts." [Curtis, 1986, p. 29][19] In fact, wherever architects see themselves as the heroic advocates of new ways of building, or new ways of interpreting society (as Le Corbusier certainly was to) they tend to invoke the Nietzschean idea of the *Übermensch* who transcends his circumstances to achieve the superhuman.

Heidegger's critique of the subjective-objective divide

Historicism focused on the view that socio-cultural phenomena stem from, and can be explained by, a specific historic context. Martin Heidegger went a step further by historicising the relationship of humans to nature and all that is, including ourselves – or in his terms: *our relationship to Being*. The way we relate to Being, Heidegger argues, is developing, or more precisely deteriorating over time. It is a history of an

以非理性、暴力和混乱的情绪为特征，但其特征也包括创造性的热情与激昂。尼采指出，从苏格拉底开始，阿波罗神主导着西方文化和思想，尼采要求我们重新发现艺术的"黑暗"面——例如理查德·瓦格纳的"整体艺术"，尼采盛赞瓦格纳是一位拯救者，至少是一段时间内的拯救者。尼采极其推崇艺术，不是因为它使我们通往更高层次的理想世界，而是因为他认为存在是荒谬的，唯有艺术能够让"存在的恐惧和可怖"变得可以承受。[17] 可是，这只有通过一个对抗时代品味、勇敢地走自己的路的天才的彻底颠覆传统的艺术才能实现。虽然尼采从哲学上说是一位历史主义者，但他对历史主义文化颇有微词。

尼采影响了十九世纪末期及之后的很多建筑师（和艺术家们），尤其是参与新艺术运动的建筑学家们。亨利·凡·德·威尔德（1863-1957）直接指出，尼采是其作品灵感的主要来源之一。他效仿尼采，对资产阶级文化进行了尖锐的批判，而尼采所提出的以"整体艺术"来复兴欧洲文化的观点也启发了凡·德·威尔德，这种艺术统一了形式和内容、艺术和日常生活、公共和私人身份。凡·德·威尔德在魏玛欣然建立了尼采档案馆（1902-1903），并策划了尼采体育场 Nietzsche-Stadion（1911-1913）。在美国，尼采的著作启示了路易斯·沙利文（1856-1924）的散文创作，沙利文的《"思想"的自传》和1886年的《灵感随笔》应归功于沃尔特·惠特曼的诗歌和德国浪漫主义。[18] 他用第三人称来谈论自己，尤为生动：路易斯被描写成一个英雄人物，他注定要克服其追求艺术的道路上的小障碍。另一位坚持用第三人称指代自己的建筑师是勒·柯布西耶，本名是夏尔-爱德华·让纳雷：1920年，他与画家阿梅代·奥赞方共同创办了杂志《新精神》，使用了自己的笔名。勒·柯布西耶的阅读涉猎甚广，受此影响，他的思想是复杂的，但我们知道，在二十二岁易受影响的年龄，他第一次到访巴黎，如饥似渴般读了勒南的《基督的一生》和尼采的《查拉图斯特拉如是说》。正如威廉·柯蒂斯所说的，"这是一个动荡的时期，他在自命不凡和深刻的自我怀疑之间摇摆不定。"（柯蒂斯，1986年，p．29）[19] 事实上，无论建筑师认为自己是英雄般的建筑新方法的倡导者，或是阐释社会的新方法的倡导者（例如勒·柯布西耶），他们都倾向于采用尼采的"超人"理念，即超越自身的状况实现超凡的成就。

海德格尔对于主观客观分化的评论

历史决定论着重关注的一点是，社会文化现象源于一个特定的历史背景，也可以被这个特定的历史背景所解释。马丁·海德格尔则更进一步，他为人与自然以及一切万有（包括我们自己）的关系赋予了历史意义，用他的说法就是：我们与存在的关系。海德格尔表示，我们与存在的联结方式处在发展之中，更准确地来说，是随着时间的推移不断恶化。这是一个

increasing gap between the subject and the object, between autonomous, world-less humans and a world deprived of all value that becomes something we see merely in functional terms. Modern humans lost their place in Being (thus nature, and the world) and consequently find no more meaning in their existence. And, most importantly, Heidegger would see the two opposed ways of looking at the world we have described, namely a more subject – and a more object-centred approach, as just part of this process – and something to *overcome* rather than embrace or take as a given framework. For Heidegger, the origin of this process has to be seen in ancient Greece where Western philosophy began. By raising the Socratic question of rational justification, people began to move themselves away from, and place themselves against, Being – a process that leads to modern science and technology as the ultimate attempt to dominate this world, with its associated positivistic philosophy, and this is an attempt that Heidegger regards as totalitarian in its aspiration. This critique explains an important aspect of his philosophy, namely a prevailing anti-rationalism. Precisely because of the negative effects of Western philosophy, he is critical of the ideal of reason that, according to Heidegger, lies at its heart and culminates in the Enlightenment.[20] His own philosophy is designed to explore new manners of reflection that overcome this alienation. Heidegger aims at nothing less than regaining a unity of man with Being through a radically different way of thinking. For the committed Heideggerian the whole ambition of this section, which describes various theoretical attitudes in relation to architecture, is already ludicrous because it is inevitably circumscribed by post-enlightenment pre-conceptions about what theory is. Heidegger's resulting methodological innovations are the cause of considerable animosity. While some argue that he opens a new way to think more deeply (and to understand Being more adequately), by departing from the traditional manner of reasoning, others oppose Heidegger for exactly this reason. His way of presenting his ideas does not allow for the normal standards of critical control or debate. It is held against him that instead of presenting arguments, he merely "reveals" some ideas he happens to have, or refers to other visionary prophets and poets like Hölderlin.

Based upon this general account of an increasing alienation of humans and nature (or of Being), Heidegger developed a highly influential critique of modern technology. His central point is that we must go beyond the traditional view of seeing technical artefacts as mere instruments that support humans in achieving their goals. For Heidegger technology is itself a metaphysical problem, because it is the culmination of the very form of reasoning that has forgotten what Being is. Technology is the embodiment of a wrong philosophy. The essence of technology – Heidegger belongs to the phenomenological school that asks for the essence of things – is to confront (*stellen*) nature, to functionalize it and to reduce it to a mere object of manipulation. Ultimately all world becomes an artefact.

What does this mean for architecture? For Heidegger, this negative development includes the way we build and comes to its peak in technocratic Modernism, the merely functional interpretation of buildings being one of its clearest expressions. Modern

主体和客体之间、自主的无世界性的人类与被剥夺了所有价值、仅剩功能层面的世界之间隔阂越来越大的历史。现代人丧失了他们在存在当中的位置（也因此丧失了在自然以及世界中的位置），从而不能再找到他们生存的意义。最为重要的是，关于我们所描述的两种截然相反的看待世界的方法，即一个偏重以主体为中心的方法和一个偏重以客体为中心的方法，海德格尔认为它们是人类丧失其生存意义的过程中的一部分，是需要解决的问题，而不应作为一种给定的框架予以接受或采纳。对于海德格尔来说，这一过程起源于西方哲学的发源地古希腊。人们在提出苏格拉底式的理性证成的问题时，就开始远离存在，并将自己与存在对立起来，这一过程中产生了现代科学和技术，这是人们试图主宰这一世界的终极尝试。现代科学和技术以及相关的实证主义哲学，被海德格尔看作是人们渴求极权主义的一种举动。这一批判说明了海德格尔哲学思想的一个重要方面，即他所推崇的反理性主义。准确地来说，在海德格尔看来，对理性的推崇是西方哲学的核心，并在启蒙运动时期达到顶峰，而正是基于西方哲学所带来的消极影响，他对崇尚理性持批判的态度。[20] 他自身的哲学思想旨在探索能够克服这一异化的新的思考方式。海德格尔的目的是通过一种极为不同的思维方式，重新获得人和存在的统一性。本章节描述了关于建筑的各种理论态度，对于坚定的海德格尔派来说，这一章节的整体立意不可避免地受到了后启蒙时代关于理论是什么的预设概念的限制。海德格尔所带来的方法学创新引发了相当大的敌意。尽管一些人表示海德格尔通过偏离传统论证方法的途径，开启了一条更加深入的思考方式（也是更为充分理解存在的方式），其他人恰恰因为这个原因反对海德格尔。他表达自己观点的方式并未考虑到临界控制点或辩论的常规标准。人们指责他只是"透露"了他碰巧拥有的一些观点，或者参考了诸如荷尔德林这样的有远见卓识的预言者和诗人，而不是在阐述论点。

　　基于人和自然（或者存在）越来越异化的这一概述，海德格尔针对现代科技提出了一种具有高度影响力的批判。他的中心观点是我们必须超越那种将技术产品仅仅视为支持人们达成其目标的工具的这一传统观点。对海德格尔来说，技术本身是一个形而上学的问题，因为技术是已经忘记何谓存在的论证形式的巅峰。科技是错误哲学思想的具象化。科技的本质——海德格尔属于追寻事物本质的现象主义学派——是对抗（stellen）自然，使其功能化，并将其弱化为一个被操纵的对象。最终整个世界会沦为一个人工产物。

这对建筑来说意味着什么？海德格尔认为，这种消极的发展也体现在我们的建筑方式中，其巅峰是技术统治论的现代主义，仅仅对建筑进行功能性的解读是这一消极发展的最明显的表现形式之一。现代建

architecture seems just part and parcel of the ongoing alienation of man from Being. To understand a house as merely "a machine for living in" is for Heidegger an "absurdity" that shows all too well the "groundlessness that dominates today's thinking and understanding".[21] In his 1951 lecture *Building Dwelling Thinking* – arguably one of the most influential texts for the twentieth century philosophy of architecture – Heidegger outlined what architecture should be like in order to go beyond the malaise of modernity, or, more precisely, to return to a lost unity of man and Being.

In Heidegger's words, man has lost the ability to dwell and to build for dwelling, not mere "living": "The essence of building is letting dwell" [Heidegger, 1951, p. 361]. And dwelling is seen as a form of being in this lost unity that is not opposed to Being – and which includes the right way of thinking (thus the title of the lecture). Heidegger posits four elements – the "fourfold" – as essential to good dwelling, for bringing "dwelling to the fullness of its nature", namely "earth, sky, divinities and mortals" [Heidegger, 1951, p. 351]. Basically, all four elements stand for a relation with Being that does not suffer from the split of modern subjectivism. The "earth" means to have a right, non-functional relation to plants, animals or water, the "sky" expresses our relation to light and the passage of time. The "divinities" are understood as unseen yet inherent beings in the world around us that give it its own meaning. By "the mortals" Heidegger means humans and their ability to reflect upon their death; only humans who fully understand their mortality have found an access to Being – and only they can dwell if they place themselves in relation to the earth and sky, and if they realise that the divinities reveal themselves through and in the world.

Heidegger's influence on twentieth century architectural reflection and architecture has been enormous.[22] And he rightly reminds us that how we build cannot be reduced to functional considerations or the applications of bourgeois decoration – building is altogether a "deeper" issue. Such a philosophical awareness had become rare in the first half of the twentieth century, a time dominated by specialized architectural theory and European Modernity. Most importantly, Heidegger pointed to the deep link between our ideas and thoughts, the way we live and the manner in which we build. The demands, for example, that architecture should be sensitive towards different cultures and their ways of life influenced the critic Kenneth Frampton (born 1930), who based his appeal for a *Critical Regionalism* directly on Heidegger's work [Frampton, 1983]: the primary thesis being that we should build with more sensitivity to a place, its culture and context. Already, in his widely-read *Modern Architecture, a Critical History*, Frampton had used Heidegger in the final paragraph. He had been praising the buildings of Alvar Aalto, as an example of work which, in comparison to much twentieth century design, is better in photographs than actuality, and concludes:

> Against his inspiring achievement, the present tendency of modern building to be devoid of content, to be reduced, so to speak, through the way it is built, returns us to the Heideggerian challenge that building, dwelling, cultivating and being were once indivisible. [Frampton, 1980]

筑似乎只是人远离自然的持续异化过程的一部分。将房屋仅视为"供居住的机器"，对于海德格尔来说是"极为荒谬的"，它淋漓尽致地体现了"主宰当今思维和理解的无根性"。[21] 海德格尔1951年名为 "建造，居住，思考" 的演讲可以说是关于二十世纪建筑哲学的最有影响力的言论之一。在此次演讲中，他概述了如果要超越现代性的难题，或者更为准确地说，要回归已经丧失的人和存在的统一性，建筑应该是什么样子的。

　　用海德格尔的话来说，人们已经失去了栖居的能力和建造栖居之处的能力，而不仅仅是"生活"的能力："建筑的本质是容许栖居"[海德格尔，1951，p.361]。栖居被视为在已经丧失的统一性中的一种存在形式，它并不与存在相悖，其中也包含了正确的思维方式（这因此成为海德格尔演讲的题目）。海德格尔设定了良好住所必不可少的四种要素，即"四重性"，将"栖居引向其本质的圆满"，即"土地，天空，神灵和凡人"[海德格尔，1951年，p. 351]。基本上，这四个要素代表着和存在的一种关系，这种关系并未受到现代主观主义裂变的影响。"土地"意味着和植物、动物或者水有一种恰当的、非功能性的关系，"天空"表达了我们与光和时间推移的关系。"神灵"可以看作是在我们周围的世界里看不见但固有的存在，并赋予我们周围的世界以意义。对于"凡人"，海德格尔意指人类及他们反思死亡的能力；只有那些能够充分理解其生命有限性的人们才能发现通向存在的道路。人们只有将自身与土地和天空联系起来，只有意识到神灵藉由这个世界、在这个世界上的存在和显现，才能够栖居。

　　海德格尔对二十世纪的建筑反思和建筑学影响巨大。[22] 他恰当地提醒了我们，我们建造住所的方式不能沦为对功能性因素的考量，或者对中产阶级装饰的堆砌——建筑从根本上来说是一个"更深刻"的问题。这种哲学意识在二十世纪上半叶是很难得的，因为那个时期是由专业化的建筑理论和欧洲现代风格主导的。最重要的是，海德格尔指出了我们的观点和想法、我们的生活方式以及我们的建造方式之间的深层连结。举例而言，他要求建筑应反映不同的文化及不同的生活方式，这影响了批评家肯尼斯·弗兰普顿（1930年出生），他直接在海德格尔著作的基础上提出了批判性地域主义[弗兰普顿，1983]：其基本论点是，我们的建筑要对一个地方、这个地方的文化和周围环境有更多的敏感性。弗兰普顿的《现代建筑——批判史》一书读者甚众，他在该书最后一段引用了海德格尔的观点。弗兰普顿对阿尔瓦·阿尔托的建筑作品一直称赞有加，认为对方的建筑和很多二十世纪的设计相比，在照片上比实际更出色，弗兰普顿的结论是：

> 　　与他（注：阿尔瓦·阿尔托）鼓舞人心的成就相悖的是，现代建筑的当下趋势是日益空洞无物，日益弱化，这种趋势在建造方式中体现出来，可以说这让我们重返海德格尔抛出的问题，即建造、栖居、耕作和存在曾经一度是不可分割的。[弗兰普顿，1980]

The thinking of the Norwegian architectural theorist and historian, Christian Nor-berg-Schulz, illustrates the continuing influence of Heidegger's thought in the late twentieth century. He changed his position from that of his *Intentions in Architecture,* which is a version of Alberti, translating the Vitruvian *firmitas, commoditas* and *venus-tas* into technics, function and form [Norberg-Schulz, 1966]. In his later books he moves towards an existential theory (*Existence, Space and Architecture* [Norberg-Schulz, 1971]) and with *Genius Loci: Towards a Phenomenology of Architecture* [Nor-berg-Schulz, 1990] Norberg-Schultz made the concept of place a major criterion, and not something that can be subsumed into the other Vitruvian categories, explicitly invoking the authority of Heidegger. Other architectural theorists who have devel-oped a Heideggerian position include Karsten Harries and Dalibor Vesely [Harries, 1975; 1997; Vesely, 2004].

Practising architects may be more influenced by teachers who have their own practice, however. One such is the Finnish architect, Juhani Pallasmaa (1936 -). As a young man, under the influence of the rationalist architect, Aulis Blomstedt, he had been critical of the apparently intuitive and irrational work of his compatriot Alvar Aalto. But in the 1960s he moved towards a phenomenological position, indebted to Merleau-Ponty and Heidegger: architectural creation is not a matter merely of the mind, it involves the whole person. In a lecture in Helsinki, he quotes a statement by the sculptor, Henry Moore:

> This is what the sculptor must do. He must strive continually to think of, and use, form in its full spatial completeness. He gets the solid shape, as it were, inside his head – he thinks of it, whatever its size, as if he were holding it completely enclosed in the hollow of his hand. He mentally visualizes a complex form from all round itself; he knows while he looks at one side what the other side is like; he identifies himself with its center of gravity, its mass, its weight; he realizes its volume, and the space that the shape displaces in the air. [Moore, 1966; cited in Pallasmaa, 2005]

Architects should conceive of buildings in the same way. Pallasmaa justifies his advocacy of an empathetic method of design by reference to Heidegger:

> No wonder Martin Heidegger writes of the thinking hand: 'The hand is infinitely different from all the grasping organs [...] Every motion of the hand in every one of its works carries itself through the element of thinking, every bearing of the hand bears itself in that element. All the work of the hand is rooted in thinking.' [Heideg-ger, 1938, p.357; cited in Pallasmaa, 2005]

It is significant that it is easier to analyse the experience of architecture in Heideg-gerian or post-Heideggerian terms than to translate such thinking into prescriptions for design. Poetically thinking about shelter and its meaning does not tell architects directly how they can improve their work, and much critical writing merely illustrates buildings that are moving examples from the past, by architects who have probably

海德尔格的思想在二十世纪晚期持续发挥着影响力，这在挪威建筑理论学家和历史学家克里斯蒂安•诺尔伯格•舒尔茨的思想中有所体现。舒尔茨先前在《建筑的意向》一书中的立场是阿尔伯蒂式的，他将罗马建筑师维特鲁威提出的"稳固、实用和外型美观"解释为技术、功能和形式[诺尔伯格•舒尔茨，1966]，但他后来改变了立场。在其后续著作中，他逐步发展出一种存在性理论（《存在•空间•建筑》[诺尔伯格•舒尔茨，1971]），在《场所精神：迈向建筑现象学》[诺尔伯格•舒尔茨，1990]这本书里，舒尔茨显然借用了海德格尔的权威学说，使得场所概念成为了一个主要标准，而且维特鲁威理论的任何其他范畴都无法涵盖这一概念。支持海德格尔观点的建筑理论学家还包括卡斯腾•哈里斯和达利波•维斯里 [哈里斯，1975；1997；维斯里，2004]。

但是，对于从业建筑师来说，他们可能更容易受那些有实践经验的老师们的影响。其中一个例子是芬兰建筑师尤哈尼•帕拉斯马（1936-）。作为一个年轻人，在理性主义建筑师奥利斯•布隆史泰特的影响下，他一度对同为芬兰人的阿尔瓦•阿尔托的看似直观主义和非理性的作品持批判态度。但在二十世纪六十年代，帕拉斯马受到梅洛•庞蒂和海德格尔的影响，开始转向现象学的立场：建筑创作不仅仅是头脑的产物，它涉及人的全部。在赫尔辛基的一次讲座中，他引用了雕塑家亨利•摩尔的话：

> 以下是雕塑家必须要做的事情。他必须不断努力地思考具备全部空间完整性的形式，并使用这种形式。他在脑海里勾勒出雕塑的完整外形，他不断地琢磨它，不论雕塑的尺寸多大，就好像把它握在自己的手掌心里一样。他构想着雕塑的方方面面；当他看着雕塑的这一面，也非常清楚另一面是什么样子；他对雕塑的重心、质量和重量了然于胸；他了解它的体积，以及雕塑形状占据的空间。[摩尔，1966年；帕拉斯马引用，2005年]

建筑师也应该以这样的方式去构想建筑。帕拉斯马援引了海德格尔的观点来支持他提倡的情感共鸣式的设计方法：

> 难怪马丁•海德格尔如此描述一只思考的手：'手与所有的抓取器官是极为不同的[…] 在创作每一件作品时，手的每一次移动、每一个姿态都传递着思考的元素。手的所有工作都植根于思考。'[海德格尔，1938年，第357页；帕拉斯马引用，2005年]

很重要的一点是，以海德格尔或者后海德格尔的术语来分析建筑经验较为容易，而要将这些想法转化为设计方法，则比较困难。对居所及其意义做诗意的思考，并不能直截了当地让建筑师们知道如何改进其作品，诸多的批判性文字展示的是古老时代的动人的建筑范例，而这些建筑的建造者可能

never heard of Heidegger. But Heidegger's critique of an extreme technocratic functionalism surely deserves attention: by common consent modern architecture often neglected human needs as well as aesthetic conventions.

However, Heidegger's approach is also the object of much critique. Surely his position leads towards a nostalgic romanticism well beyond the needs of the seven billion people that want a decent place to live. And others have argued that Heidegger's thinking in relation to architecture fails to account for social and economic realities even in privileged societies [Leach, 2002]. Although he expressly rejects any nostalgia[23] and claims not to want to return to traditional Black Forest farmhouses,[24] it is striking that all his examples of successful dwelling stem from a pre-twentieth century era. Similarly, his strict condemnation of all functional reasoning can hardly convince.[25]

But more profoundly, we might critique Heidegger for some inconsistency in his critical account of the decline of European culture. According to his diagnosis we are at the end of a sad story of forgetting Being – but then it is neither clear how good dwelling and a right relationship to the fourfold should be possible at all in our times, nor where Heidegger's own place in the European history of ideas should be. (Why, after so much decline, is it suddenly possible to have all the direct insights that he claims to have?) Unsurprisingly Heidegger's critique of particular phenomena (for example of the technocratic thinking endemic in modernity) has influenced philosophers and architects more profoundly than his general metaphysics of history.[26]

The post-metaphysical age

Anyone thinking and writing about architecture in the twentieth and twenty-first centuries has had to come to terms with the fact that the meanings that used to be embedded within the fabric of cities and their buildings have disappeared. If a Gothic cathedral was once a "sermon in stone", what can be deduced about our society from the major constructions of our own times? The iconography of a complex of buildings such as Le Corbusier's capitol at the new Indian city of Chandigarh was a self-consciously personal one. He included a vast "open hand" sculpture, and inscriptions describing the cycle of the sun and moon, but the buildings themselves have forms that refer more generally either to the idea of the technology of a "new" nation (the parliament building's profile is based on power station cooling towers) or are fashioned in response to technical problems, such as the creation of shade on the facades of the buildings, which is achieved by means of the "brise-soleil" on many of them, or the vast canopy over the law courts. Admirers believe that the sculptural forms that result have universal relevance and argue that they refer at a deeper level to primary existential experience. The work of Mircea Eliade [1971] would suggest that the very act of establishing a site in the landscape and the creation of a place under the sun can carry transcultural embedded meaning, and Christian Norberg-Schulz's

从未听说过海德格尔。但海德格尔对于极端的技术统治型的实用主义的批判确实值得关注：人们公认，现代建筑常常忽略了人的需要以及审美传统。

然而，海德格尔的方法也是很多人批判的对象。无疑，海德格尔的观点通向一种怀旧的浪漫主义，远远超越了希望有体面住处的七十亿人的需求。还有些人认为，海德格尔关于建筑的见解并未考虑社会和经济方面的实际情况，哪怕是特权社会的实际情况也未予考虑［利奇，2002］。尽管他明确拒绝任何怀旧，[23] 并声称不想回到传统的黑森林农舍，[24] 但很明显的一点是，他所有关于栖居的成功范例都来自二十世纪以前。同样地，他对所有功能性理性辨析的严厉谴责也很难说服人说他是拒绝怀旧的。[25]

而一个更深刻的问题是，我们可能会评论海德格尔对欧洲文化衰落的批判性论述中出现的不一致现象。根据他的判断，人们忘记了"存在"，而我们就处在这个悲伤故事的结尾，但是在我们这个时代，栖居到底能有多好，与四要素的恰当关系是什么样的，以及海德格尔在欧洲思想史上的位置如何，这些都不是很清楚。（为什么在经历如此大的文化衰落之后，还可能出现海德格尔声称拥有的那些直入人心的见解？）与他的历史形而上学通论相比，海德格尔对于特定现象（例如现代特有的技术统治论思想）的批判对哲学家和建筑学家的影响更为深刻，这也不足为奇。[26]

后形而上学时代

任何人在思考和撰写二十世纪和二十一世纪的建筑学时都不得不对一个事实妥协，即城市及其建筑物的结构中曾经蕴含的意义已经消失。如果一座哥特式教堂曾经能够"以石布道"，那么从我们这个时代的重要建筑物中能演绎出关于我们这个社会的哪些东西？一个建筑群—例如勒·柯布西耶设计的印度新城市昌迪加尔议会大楼—展示了个人的自我意识的意象。柯布西耶的设计里包括一个巨大的"张开的手"雕塑，以及描绘太阳和月亮周期的铭文，但这个建筑群本身所包含的形式要么更广泛地指向"新"国家的技术理念（议会大厦的剖面以发电站冷却塔为基础），要么是为了解决技术问题而设计的，例如在建筑物外立面增加遮棚，这参考了很多建筑的"遮阳板"或法庭上方的巨大顶篷而得以实现。推崇者们相信，由此产生的雕塑形式具有普遍意义，他们认为这些雕塑形式在更深的层次上涉及到了基本的存在经验。米尔恰·伊利亚德［1971］的作品表明，在大地之上设立一处场所或在太阳底下创造一处场所，这种行为本身就能够传达一种跨文化的内在含义，克里斯蒂安·诺尔伯格·舒尔茨的

Existence, Space and Architecture similarly holds out this hope [Norberg-Schulz, 1971].

But others are less optimistic. The American planner Melvin Webber (1920- 2006) coined the expression "non-place urban realm" in 1965 to refer to the fact that previous understandings of urban fabric had been made redundant in an age of rapid transportation and communication: community was no longer defined by propinquity so that fantasies about reconstructing the city along the models of Europe were pure nostalgia. And in a series of well-documented conferences entitled ANY, a number of architects and critics in the closing years of the twentieth century debated the loss of traditional architectural certainties: not only its material solidity, but also its reference to the specifics of location, stable definition of function, hierarchies of use, and modes of formal signification were all called into question. The final conference was addressed by Rem Koolhaas, who presented two projects: a new headquarters for Universal City in Los Angeles and four new Prada stores. As the critic of the New York Times described it:

> The modern aesthetic was theoretically objective. It evoked the rational mechanics of technology and industrial production. A Koolhaas design may employ modern forms and materials – glass, grids, sculptural abstraction – but does not organize these elements into a neutral, functionalist container. There are subjectivisms along the way. Floors morph into ramps, spirals into squares; escalators expand space as if through a camera lens. Reason is contorted by desire. We seem always to be slipping through some porous membrane, back and forth between semipublic and semiprivate space, as if no fixed boundaries divide environment from self. [Muschamp, 2000]

There is a further critique of traditional (rational) metaphysics that has been of particular importance for architecture: Post-modernism, understood as a loosely connected set of ideas and cultural (architectural, artistic and philosophical) trends that lack a clear tenet, and consciously do so. The American architect Robert Venturi suggested that the times require a shift of attitude:

> At the beginning of this century you could be Bernard "Sure" – you could be a very strong artist and take unambiguous stands. The good guys and the bad guys – it was obvious who they were. Now, I think, intelligent people are no longer that sure of simple answers and drastic actions, and this is reflected in the fact that there are inevitable contradictions and ambiguities in the work.[27]

Thus Post-modernism rejects all "grand stories" and coherent overall worldviews. One could describe it as scepticism that has been turned against itself: if there are no universal truths to be found, then even this judgement – namely that there is no universal truth – cannot be a universal truth.[28] What we call "truth" is then not much more than the views of any one time, as for example Michel Foucault and Richard Rorty argue, resulting from both a conscious struggle for power and influence, and sub-conscious

《存在、空间和建筑》也表明了同样的愿景 [诺尔伯格•舒尔茨，1971年]。

但其他人并没有那么乐观。美国规划师麦尔文•韦伯（1920—2006）于1965年首次提出"非空间的城市领域"，指的是这一事实：人们以前对于城市结构的理解在快速交通和通信时代已成为多余：社区不再根据空间的邻近性来界定，因此那些根据欧洲模式重建城市的幻想只是纯粹在怀旧而已。在有充分的文件记载的ANY系列会议上，一些建筑师和评论家在二十世纪的最后几年里围绕传统的建筑确定性的丧失进行了辩论：建筑作为物质层面的坚实存在，它与所处的具体环境的关联，关于功能的确切定义，使用的层次结构，以及用形式传递内涵的种种范式，都受到了质疑。在最后一场会议上，雷姆•库哈斯作了发言，展示了两个项目：环球影城在洛杉矶的新总部，以及四个普拉达品牌新门店。纽约时报评论员对此评论如下：

> 现代美学从理论上说是客观的。它使人联想到技术和工业生产的理性力学。库哈斯的设计或许使用了一些现代形式和材料，包括玻璃、格栅、抽象雕塑，但并不是将这些元素糅合到一个中立的、功能主义学派的容器里。主观意识是一直都在的。地板变为斜坡，螺旋变为方块；自动扶梯延展了空间，就像通过相机镜头观看的效果。理性因为欲望而扭曲。我们似乎总是在半公开空间和半私密空间之间来来回回，就像穿过多孔薄膜一样，仿佛在环境和自我之间并没有固定的边界。[马斯卡姆，2000]

传统（理性）形而上学受到进一步的批判，虽然它对建筑学影响极大：后现代主义被理解为一系列缺乏清晰原则的、联系松散的观点和文化（包括建筑、艺术和哲学）的潮流。美国建筑师罗伯特•文丘里认为，这个时代需要态度的转变：

> 在本世纪之初，你可能是一个态度强势的艺术家，立场毫不含糊。好人和坏人之间的分别非常明显。我认为，现在智慧的人们不再确信简单的答案和激烈的行为，这通过一个事实反映出来，即作品中不可避免的矛盾和不确定性。[27]

因此，后现代主义拒绝一切"精彩故事"和一致的整体世界观。这可以称之为以己之矛攻己之盾的怀疑主义：如果未发现普世真理，那么即使是没有普世真理的这一判断，也不可能是一条普世真理。[28] 我们所称的"真理"也不过是每个时代的各种观点而已，正如米歇尔•福柯和理查德•罗蒂宣称的，这些观点来自为权力和影响力而展开的有意识的争斗，以及潜意识里的

needs and desires. Hans Blumenberg and Peter Sloterdijk suggest that these "truths" fulfil certain social and psychological functions, for example stabilising cultures and communities – but that there is no truth in any more profound, objective sense.

The Western idea of *reason* as a unifying faculty, universal to all mankind, is seen as an essentialist illusion: the enlightenment optimism about rationality, and its further development by modernist functionalism, gets "deconstructed" – it is merely the apotheosis of the hegemonic ambition of Western culture and should be abandoned. Consequently, Post-modernism emphasises contradiction, ambiguity, diversity, and interconnectedness; to seek order, structure, let alone meaning in this world is precisely to succumb to the rejected point of view of a universal reason.[29] This explains why for Post-modernism there seems no reason to take the departure from objective truth (or values, or meaning) particularly seriously: "If *sub specie aeternitatis* there is no reason to believe that anything matters, then that does not matter either, and we can approach our absurd lives with irony instead of heroism or despair" [Nagel, 1979, p. 23]. While previous forms of nihilism gave much weight to the 'heroic' or superhuman task of overcoming the grand illusions and of creating one's own values or meaning, for Post-modernism even this endeavour is regarded as vain. Nihilism becomes an ironic play – Post-modernism promises a light approach towards a world and existence without gravity and goal; it shows the *bearable lightness of being*.

A clear target for architectural post-modernists was the orthodoxy of CIAM, the *Congrès Internationaux des Architectes Modernes*, a group of avant-garde architects. In August 1933 the fourth and most famous meeting of CIAM took place, on the steamship *Patras II* voyaging to Athens, beginning and ending in Marseilles. The meeting was dominated by the powerful persona and polemic of Le Corbusier. Out of it was to emerge the *Charter of Athens*, though it was not published until ten years later, a devastatingly reductive prescription for the development of cities, distinguishing the functions of work, leisure, and recreation, connected by systems of circulation, as problems to be "solved" by rational town planning. Paragraph 16 for example runs:

> Structures built along transportation routes and around their intersections are detrimental to habitation because of noise, dust and noxious gases.

Having eliminated the street, "high buildings, set far apart from one another, must free the ground for broad verdant areas" (paragraph 29). "The practice of using styles of the past", we are told in paragraph 70, "on aesthetic pretexts for new structures in historic areas has harmful consequences. Neither the continuation of such practices nor the introduction of such initiatives will be tolerated in any form." [Eardley, 1973]

Such dogmatic certainty about the inadequacy of traditional forms of planning and architecture called into question the whole concept of "rational" architecture and planning. Post-modernist architecture advocated an unapologetically diverse Aesthetics, for example by using traditional elements, historical forms, or surface ornaments from different styles.

需求和欲望。汉斯·布鲁门贝格和彼得·斯洛特迪基克建议 ，这些"真理"满足了某些特定的社会和心理功能，例如使文化和社会得以稳定，但从任何更为深刻和客观的意义上来讲，并不存在真理。

　　西方观点认为理性是一种普适于全人类的统一的天赋，这种观点是一种本质上的幻觉：启蒙运动时期对理性的乐观态度，以及现代功能主义对理性的进一步发展，最终使得理性"被解构"。理性只是西方文化称霸野心的发展巅峰，它应该被废弃。因此，后现代主义强调矛盾、模糊、多样性和相互关联性；普世理性已经遭到驳斥，对秩序与结构的寻求正是普世理性遭驳斥的关键所在，更不必说寻求世界的意义了。[29] 这解释了为何对于后现代主义来说，似乎没有理由把严重背离客观真相（或价值、意义）看得那么重要："如果说在永恒形相之下，没有理由相信任何事情是重要的，那么这件事本身也不重要，我们可以一种讽刺的态度来看待我们荒诞的生活，而非用英雄主义的方式看待或感到悲观失望"[内格尔，1979，第23页]。尽管之前各种形式的虚无主义很看重一个"英雄"般的或超人般的任务，即超越宏伟的幻觉并创造个人自身的价值或意义，对于后现代主义来说，即使是这种努力也被视为徒劳。虚无主义成为一种颇具讽刺的表演——后现代主义允诺了一种通向世界和存在的轻松路径，这个世界和存在没有重力、没有目标；它展现了"不能承受的生命之轻"。

　　后现代主义建筑师们追求的一个清晰目标是先锋派建筑师群体CIAM（Congrès Internationaux des Architectes Modernes）所代表的正统思想。在1933年8月，CIAM举行了第四届会议，也是最著名的一次会议，这次会议在蒸汽轮船帕特雷二世（Patras II）上举办，从法国马赛出发前往雅典，再返回马赛。勒·柯布西耶强有力的个性和辩论主导了这场会议。此次会议达成了《雅典宣言》，尽管在十年之后才得以公开发布，但该宣言提供了极其令人难忘的关于城市发展的简化方式，城市发展要区分工作、休闲和娱乐的功能，彼此由各个循环系统联结，需要通过理性的城镇规划"解决"种种问题。例如第16段表示：

　　　　由于噪音、灰尘和有害气体，沿着运输线路和围绕运输线路交叉口建
　造的建筑物不利于居住。

　　除去街道之外，"彼此远离的高耸的建筑物必须把地面解放出来，用作广阔的绿地"（第29段）。第70段告诉我们，"在历史区域以美学为名仿造过去的风格搭建新建筑，会引发不良的后果。不论是延续已有的工程还是启动新的项目，这种做法都不应被容忍。"[厄德利，1973]

　　由于后现代主义固执地认为规划和建筑的传统形式存在不足，使得"理性"建筑和规划的整个概念受到了质疑。后现代主义建筑倡导一种不容置疑的多元化美学，例如，它可以通过使用传统元素、历史形式、或不同风格的外在装饰来实现。

More obviously, Post-modernism gives up the ideal of any *one* point of reference. There is no ideal of unity left, no order to be discovered. If the world is ultimately diverse and ambiguous, then this requires an architecture that is based upon such ideas. While Historicism still hoped for a rational answer to the question of style, there is no longer a right answer to be expected – it is left to the aesthetic taste of the architect. Even the concept of a coherent style seems to suggest too much consistency in an ultimately pluralistic world; that is why Post-modernism does not revive a single style but only fragments thereof.

The general rejection of all universal values, moral or aesthetic, is mirrored in aesthetic productions: Robert Venturi, amongst others, seeks to avoid traditional evaluations. In his 1972 book *Learning from Las Vegas*, he celebrates the ordinary and commonplace architecture of, for example, a shopping mall [Venturi and Scott-Brown, 1972]. Venturi argues for buildings that quite explicitly display their symbolism. Paradoxically, under modernist orthodoxy where decoration was prohibited, the whole building was distorted in order to create a symbol.[30] But the syntax of this symbolism was so arcane that the buildings were often illiterate in their own terms and unintelligible to the layman, merely huge pieces of sculptural decoration. Venturi, using the precedent of the Las Vegas strip, advocates, in most instances, a "billboard" architecture where the functions were accommodated in quite ordinary sheds and the signs were applied up in front where it showed. This is the procedure, he claims, in mannerist and baroque churches and on the west fronts of gothic cathedrals. But sheds and some applied decoration are all that late twentieth-century budgets will afford in any case. The prescription is therefore both populist (in adopting the ordinary pattern of the Las Vegas strip), and ironic, to those who can read the irony. And the reason for the irony, ultimately, is the context in which architects of the late twentieth century inevitably find themselves. As Venturi explained in his earlier *Complexity and Contradiction in Architecture*, society no longer values architecture; it spends its big money on armaments, or technological gadgets:

> The architect who would accept his role as combiner of significant old clichés – valid banalities in new contexts – as his condition within a society that directs its best efforts, its big money and its elegant technologies elsewhere, can ironically express in this indirect way a true concern for society's inverted scale of values. [Venturi, 2006].

更明显的是，后现代主义放弃了关于任何统一参照物的理想。不再有统一的理想，也没有秩序之说。如果世界归根结底是多元化的、模棱两可的，那么建筑就需要以这些观点为基础。尽管历史主义仍期待着关于风格问题得到一个理性的答案，但它再也无法得到一个正确的答案，因为风格问题是由建筑师的美学品味决定的。即使是风格一致这种概念在我们这个多元化的世界里都显得过于强调一致性；这就是为什么后现代主义没有复兴任何一种单一的风格，而只是复兴了风格的碎片。

对于所有（道德的或美学的）普世价值的全然排斥，通过美学作品映现出来：罗伯特•文丘里等人，试图避免传统的评判方式。在其1972年撰述的《学习拉斯维加斯》一书中，他称赞了购物中心这样普通寻常的建筑[文丘里和斯科特•布朗，1972]。文丘里支持清楚展现其象征意义的建筑物。而矛盾的是，现代主义的正统观念禁止使用装饰，在这种情况下，整个建筑物为创造一种象征而扭曲了自身。[30] 但是，该象征主义的结构形式又如此晦涩难懂，以至于建筑物自身通常是晦涩的，外行人更难以理解，看上去不过是大片的雕饰而已。文丘里援引了拉斯维加斯大道这一先例，提倡在大多数情况下采用"告示牌"式的建筑，它以相当普通的棚式建筑物来承载其功能，指示牌则在建筑正面予以展示。他表示，倡导风格主义的巴洛克式教堂，以及哥特式教堂的西侧正面，都采用了这种方式。但棚式建筑和那些附加装饰是二十世纪晚期的预算所能负担的全部。因此，这种方式（采纳拉斯维加斯大道的普通样式）是平民化的，而对于那些能够读懂其中反讽的人来说则颇具讽刺意味。它之所以具有讽刺意味，归根结底是因为二十世纪末期建筑师无法逃脱的时代背景。正如文丘里在其早期的《建筑的复杂性和矛盾性》一书中所讲，社会不再重视建筑，而是将大量金钱用于武器装备或者技术设备上：

> 这个社会将大量的精力、金钱和尖端技术用在了建筑之外的其他地方，在这样的背景下，如果建筑师们接受自己扮演拼装者的角色，去拼接显赫而俗套的旧有风格—即在新环境里仍然适用的陈规习俗，那么他也能够以这种间接的方式颇具讽刺地表达对于社会颠倒的价值标准的真实关切。[文丘里，2006]

Ethics

Ethical reflection on architecture[31]

Put in most general terms, Ethics is that branch of philosophy which deals with distinctions between right and wrong in human affairs, in particular with the evaluation of human intentions and character traits, of actions and their consequences. But Ethics can also investigate products of human activities like institutions, artworks or technical artefacts.

In order to investigate the ethical side of architecture more closely, we must be aware of two important ethical distinctions. Neither is specific to the Ethics of Architecture, but of general importance for Ethics in general – and often confused in texts on architectural Ethics.

We need to differentiate between, one the one hand, *facts* about buildings and, on the other hand, guiding *ideas* – values, norms, standards or the like (either ones that are held by a culture or person, or those that we subscribe to ourselves and thus apply for an ethical evaluation). "Facts" in architecture include the material used (for example: stained glass), the energy required for heating, or the style in which a building is designed. All of this, guiding ideas and facts, can be described without giving an evaluation of a building – but it will have to be its basis. Ethics thus has a *descriptive* side to it, when it records the norms and values of a culture or tradition. And Ethics can be a *normative* discipline that evaluates phenomena and tells people what to do. Both aspects are of profound relevance for architecture. On the one hand, we can describe the values or norms that have guided architects or patrons and that have shaped their buildings. We can say, for example, that Bruno Taut (1880-1938) built the "Glass House" for the *Werkbund's* 1914 exhibition with walls out of stained glass in order to inspire a reformed society that shows "translucency" – that is the mutual openness of all humans. (To make this statement neither implies that we share his ideal nor that we believe in the transformational force of stained glass.) On the other hand, people (including architects), institutions (such as building firms) and even artefacts (such as a bridge) can be evaluated from an ethical perspective. We make normative judgements, for example, when we ask whether a building is sustainable (under the assumption that the long-term protection of the environment is morally good) or whether bribes have been paid to get a building contract (under the assumption that such bribery is immoral even in cases when it is not illegal).

伦理学

对建筑的伦理反思[31]

用最通俗的语言来说，伦理学是哲学的一个分支，它着眼于区分人类事务的对与错，特别是对人类意图、性格特质以及对其行动和后果的评估。但伦理学也可以对人类活动的产物进行审视，例如制度、艺术作品或技术产品。

为了更详尽地考察建筑的伦理层面，我们必须注意到两个重要的伦理学特征。这两者都不是建筑伦理学所特有的，而是对于一般的伦理学都具有普遍的重要意义，在关于建筑伦理学的著述中两者经常被混淆。

我们有必要对建筑物的事实以及其指导思想进行区分——后者包括价值观、规范、标准等等（既可以是某种文化或某个人所持的观念，也可以是我们已接受并用于伦理评估的观念）。建筑中的"事实"包括所使用的材料（例如彩色玻璃）、供暖所需的能源、或建筑物的设计风格。我们可以对所有这些进行描述，而无需对建筑物进行评估——但所有这些描述必然是评估的基础。因此，伦理学有其描述性的一面，记录着一种文化或传统的规范和价值观。另外，伦理学也是一门规范性的学科，对现象进行评价，并告诉人们要做什么。这两个方面都与建筑有着深刻的关联。一方面，我们可以描述那些指导着建筑师或出资人、并塑造了其建造物的价值观或规范。例如，我们可以说，布鲁诺·陶特（1880-1938）为德意志制造联盟（Werkbund）1914年的展览建造了"玻璃屋"，以彩绘玻璃作为墙体，目的是激发社会革新，提倡"透明度"，即所有人之间彼此敞开。（这一表述本身并不意味着我们认同他的理念，也不意味着我们相信彩绘玻璃具有革新的力量。）另一方面，人们（包括建筑师）、机构（例如建筑公司），甚至是人工作品（例如桥梁）都可以被我们从伦理学的角度予以评价。我们评判其规范性，例如质疑一栋建筑物是否是可持续的（出于对环境的长期保护在道德上是善的这一假设），或人们是否为了获得建筑合约而行贿（出于贿赂即使不违法也是违背道德的这一假设）。

Six relevant ethical areas

We can distinguish the following six areas that seem relevant, of which only the first refers to the building process, and all others to effects of the finished structure:

• issues of professional behaviour and interaction during the planning, designing and construction phase
• the morally acceptable or unacceptable nature of the function and use of a building
• the impact of the building on nature (broadly under the heading of what we would call "green issues")
• the impact on the health and safety of those who use the buildings
• the psychological influence on human behaviour, individually and collectively, that the building induces
• the furnishing of cultural or symbolic meanings, by choices of form, materials, colours, and aesthetic style [Rapoport, 1990]. This is the most complex of the six areas identified.

We will consider these in turn.

1. *Professional behaviour*
This area of ethical relevance is probably the dominant topic of much traditional Ethics; some would go so far to *define* Ethics as a system that regulates interactions amongst humans. And it seems that architecture as a profession is particularly vulnerable to un-ethical behaviour, mainly because so much money and so many different people are involved in any building process. There is pressure at all levels and many stakeholders are trying to exercise influence on architects. However, hardly any of the ethical rules that professional bodies seek to impose are *specific* for architects. The professional code of the Dutch Royal Society of Architects, for example, requires an architect not to break confidentiality (paragraph 3.4), and not to talk negatively about other people without informing them about it (paragraph 4.2). Both demands seem right in general for *any* interaction amongst humans.[32]

2. *Function and use of the building*
What is the building designed for – or what is it used for presently? From a moral point of view, not all usages are equally good. We will, for example, rightly criticize the function of the former Berlin Wall, and expect architects to refuse to be involved in its design. Other cases are more ambivalent: architects are often involved in the design of supermarkets, and when they arrive on the fringe of a small town local traders are affected and campaigns might be mounted to prevent the new buildings gaining permission. Architects are party to this process (they might be involved on either side).
More fundamentally, we expect buildings to function well – to be fit for their purpose – and architects who design buildings which look good but do not work are

六个相关的伦理领域

我们可以区分下述六个看似相关的领域，其中只有第一个涉及建筑的过程，其他五个都是关于建筑完成后的效果：

- 人们在规划、设计和建造期间的职业行为和互动问题
- 建筑物的功能和用途，从道德层面上属于可接受或不可接受的性质
- 建筑物对自然的影响（大致属于我们所说的"绿色议题"范围内）
- 对建筑物使用者的健康和安全的影响
- 建筑物引发的心理对人类个体和集体行为的影响
- 通过对形式、材料、颜色和美学风格的选择，建筑所展现出来的文化或象征意义[拉波波特，1990]。这是以上六个领域中最为复杂的领域。

我们将依次探讨这些领域。

1. 职业行为

这一方面的伦理问题很可能是诸多传统伦理学当中的主要课题；有些人甚至把伦理学定义为一套规范人类互动行为的制度。建筑学似乎是一项极易被不道德行为影响的职业，这主要是因为任何建筑过程都会涉及大量的金钱以及形形色色的人们参与其中。其中有来自各级的压力，许多利益相关方都试图对建筑师施加影响。不过，专业机构试图推行的那些伦理规则之中极少是只适用于建筑师的。例如，荷兰皇家建筑师学会的职业准则要求建筑师不得违背保密性要求（第3.4段），不得在未告知对方的情况下发表针对此人的负面评价（第4.2段）。这两个要求总体来说适用于人们之间的任何互动行为。[32]

2. 建筑物的功能和用途

设计一栋建筑物的目的是什么，或者它当下的用途是什么？从道德的角度来看，并非所有用途都是同样良善的。例如，我们会公允地批判柏林墙的功能，并期待建筑师们拒绝参与其设计过程。而其他案例则更具矛盾性：建筑师们常常参与超市的设计，如果超市选址在一个小城镇的周边地区，当地的商贩们都会受到影响，他们可能发起运动以阻止新建筑获批。建筑师便成为其中的当事方（他们可能是支持方，也可能是反对方）。

更重要的是，我们希望建筑物很好地发挥其作用，与设计意图相吻合。如果建筑师设计的建筑徒有其表而无法使用，这样的建筑师就

behaving more like sculptors. But we have to recognise that the intended function is not necessarily the function which the building realizes; Don Ihde rightly calls this mistaken conclusion the "designer fallacy" [Ihde, 2008]. It might be that over a period of time the original function is no longer required (as in many castles), or that it has changed its use contingently. This can even be the case in a very short time period, however. Zaha Hadid was commissioned to provide a Fire Station at Weil am Rhein in 1993 by the Vitra group, but the building's purpose was swiftly made obsolete by the construction of another building and it has been used ever since for the display of furniture; it performs this function in addition to enhancing the "brand" for which it was designed, which was equally important for her clients.[33] Evaluating the function can therefore have two objects, that originally intended and the actual realised use of a building.

3. *Impact on nature*
We live in a world that has been severely and often irreversibly damaged by technical intrusions, so that the green issue is quite rightly one of the most discussed questions in relation to architecture. Buildings have an enormous environmental impact. They are responsible for 2/5th of the world's energy consumption (and in the United States 1/6th of all energy is used for air-conditioning on hot summer days).[34] In 1999, according to the United Nations Environment Programme, construction activities were estimated to contribute over 35% of total global carbon dioxide emissions – more than any other industrial activity.[35]

The demand that our building activities should respect the carrying capacity of ecosystems is essentially ethical: the selection of the site, the building process, and the final product should not contribute to the destruction of the environment and should make minimal use of limited natural resources. Some claim that this moral imperative should over-ride all other requirements for architecture: it should not matter that a building is less comfortable for its occupants than it could be, provided it is more responsible environmentally. But views differ on precisely how this value is expressed: Pepper distinguishes between "eco-centric environmentalists" and "technocentric environmentalists", where the first group harbours ecological ideals (like recycling building materials) in order to reduce the ecological footprints of buildings, the second group strives for "smart", or highly efficient technical solutions [Pepper, 1984]. Each group profoundly disagrees on what an ideal green architecture would look like. Yet there might be even more options; in a recent paper, Simon Guy and Graham Farmer list as many as six different "logics of green buildings" or understandings of the "environment" and of how we should live in it [Guy and Farmer, 2000].

4. *Impact on health and safety of individual users*
But buildings are occupied and used by people; it is quite generally seen as a moral demand that we build with a maximum concern for the health of users and occupants. A bad sanitation system, for example, threatens the health of the inhabitants. Negative effects can also be less obvious: the lack of natural light can lead to emotional problems (Seasonal Affective Disorder). A proportion of the research in schools of architecture

更像是雕塑家了。但我们必须意识到，建筑物的原定功能并不一定是它最终实现的功能；唐•伊德将这种与初衷相悖的结果称为"设计者谬误"[伊德，2008]。有可能是经过一段时间之后不再需要建筑物的原定功能了（例如很多城堡），又或者是其用途偶然间发生了改变。功能的改变甚至会在非常短的时间内发生。扎哈•哈迪德于1993年受维特拉（Vitra）集团委托，在莱茵河畔威尔城设计建造一座消防站。但另一栋建筑物的出现很快便使得消防站的原定用途作废了。从此之后这座消防站一直被用来展示家具；除这一功能之外，它还增强了委托设计方的"品牌"效应，这对于扎哈的客户们而言也是很重要的。[33] 因此，评估建筑的功能时有两个考量对象，一个是建筑物的原始预期功能，另一个是建筑物最终实现的功能。

3. 对自然的影响

我们所处的世界由于技术的侵扰而遭到了严重破坏，这些破坏往往是不可逆的，因此在关于建筑的诸多议题中，绿色议题无疑是人们最常讨论的话题之一。建筑对环境有着巨大的影响。它们占据了全球五分之二的能源消耗（在美国，在炎热的夏天使用空调消耗了所有能源的六分之一）。[34] 联合国环境规划署表示，1999年建筑活动在全球二氧化碳的排放总量中占35%以上，比其他任何工业活动都要多。[35]

我们的建筑活动应尊重生态系统的承载能力，这个要求从本质上说是伦理性的：场地的选择、建造的过程、以及最终的作品，都不应破坏环境，并且应该最小程度地使用珍贵的自然资源。有些人认为，这一道德责任应该凌驾于对建筑的其他任何要求之上：如果一栋建筑物能够更好地保护环境，那么即使居住者住得不那么舒适也没关系。然而，关于如何精确地表达这一价值观，人们有着不同的观点：佩珀对"以生态为中心的环境保护论者"和"以技术为中心的环境保护论者"进行了区分，前者心怀生态理想（例如回收利用建筑材料）致力于减少建筑物的生态足迹，后者则追求"智能"，或是高效能的技术解决方案 [佩珀，1984]。两者对于什么是理想的绿色建筑有着严重的意见分歧。这两者以外可能还有更多不同的观点；在最近的一篇文章里，西蒙•盖伊和格雷厄姆•法默列举了六种不同的"绿色建筑的逻辑"，或者说是六种不同的对"环境"的认知以及对于我们如何在环境中生活的认知 [盖伊和法默，2000]。

4. 对个人使用者的健康和安全的影响

但是，建筑是供人居住并使用的；我们在建造时应最大程度地关注使用者和居住者的健康，这通常被视为一个道德要求。举例来说，糟糕的卫生系统会威胁到居住者的健康状况。还有一些问题对健康的负面影响可能不太明显：自然光的缺乏可能会导致情感问题（季节性情感障碍）。各建筑学院进行的研究中有一部分

is devoted to making measurements of what constitutes a good environment for people. Though there are cultural differences in different societies, it is possible to calculate aspects of comfort, in terms of temperature, humidity and rates of ventilation for example, and establish the range within which we would expect the performance of buildings to fall; if their buildings fail to meet these standards we would hold the architects responsible. And progressively we may be able to measure how a building's technical performance affects people's well-being. [36]

5. *Influence on human behaviour*
Yet a detailed explanation for *how* architecture affects us will not by itself answer the ethical issues. What is the morally right way to deal with human needs? It seems plausible that buildings must satisfy at least those needs that are essential for human well-being and whose frustration makes human beings sick. But it is by no means obvious whether buildings should satisfy all needs that we have or only some of them, or which needs under which circumstances. Especially when we look at psychological needs this becomes obvious. Sometimes, it might be morally better to modify or guide some needs than to give them much space; universal desire-satisfaction has been seen as ideal by very few ethicists. Furthermore, oversensitivity to psychological effects of architecture might lead to idyllic holiday villages for tourists and other forms of *kitsch*, understood as overly sentimental, pretentious design, calculated to have popular appeal, if we are too close to the actual wishes and dreams of people.[37] The village of Portmeirion in North Wales, built over a fifty-year period from 1925 by Clough Williams-Ellis (1883-1978), would be an example: while it pleases us on holiday, it is unlikely to do so as a permanent environment. *Kitsch* satisfies certain sentiments but does so in a partial manner. What it seems to be lacking is challenge: we might argue that truly satisfying artefacts must also *demand* something from the observer.

Without falling into the trap of naïve determinism, it seems that buildings can influence the behaviour of people in morally relevant ways. In 1951, Yamasaki, the architect of the New York World Trade Centre, designed the Pruitt-Igoe housing project for the socially disadvantaged. The 11-storey buildings which totalled 2870 apartments were heralded for their innovations, but their structures seemed to invite vandalism and crime so that no one wanted to live there. The complex got demolished after just 20 years.

Architectural designs are not only influenced by a certain idea about how human beings live and what they do, buildings can also suggest ideals to their occupants: an obvious way is to make certain actions easy and others difficult or impossible.

"Space syntax" research has indicated that not only the distance between starting point and target, but also the street layout in a city, determines the road routes people take; they prefer ways that provide visual experiences [Hillier and Lida, 2005]. And even highly private decisions like family planning seem influenced by our housing conditions [Rzchtarikova and Akkerman, 2003]. These psychological effects became a topic only after the failure of many well-intended public housing projects like Pruitt-Igoe and resulted in a new science, namely architectural psychology.[38] The architect and city

是测量人们需要的良好环境是由哪些要素构成的。尽管不同的社会存在着文化差异，但我们还是能够对建筑舒适度的各个方面进行测量，例如温度、湿度和通风率，并确立一个我们期望建筑物达到的性能标准；如果建筑物无法达到这些标准，我们将追究建筑师的责任。逐渐地，我们就可以测量一栋建筑的技术性能是如何影响着人们的生活的。

5. 对人类行为的影响

然而，关于建筑物是如何影响我们的，一个具体的答案本身并不能解答伦理层面的问题。从道德层面上看，什么才是解决人们需求的正确方式呢？人们的有些需求对于其生活健康至关重要，得不到满足的话就会生病，所以建筑物必须满足这些需求，这显然是合理的。但是建筑物是否应满足我们的所有需求，还是只满足一部分，或是在哪些情况下满足哪些需求，都完全没有明确的答案。特别是当我们关注人们的心理需求时，这种情况变得尤为明显。有时候，对人们的需求进行调整或引导，从道德层面上看可能好过于充分满足这些需求；极少有伦理学家崇尚完全的欲求满足。此外，过度关注建筑对人们产生的心理效应，可能带来的就是田园风格的游客度假村和其他形式的媚俗设计，如果我们太过迎合人们的实际愿望和梦想，这些设计会被认为是过度煽情、虚伪矫饰，精心讨好大众。[36] 位于英国北威尔士的小村庄波特梅里恩（Portmeirion）就是一个例子，它由克拉夫·威廉姆斯·埃利斯（1883-1978）设计，从1925年开工，历时半个多世纪建成：虽然这个小村庄为度假的人们带来愉悦的体验，但如果作为长久居住地，它却不大可能让人愉悦。媚俗设计满足了一定的情感需求，但也只是片面的满足。它缺失的是挑战性：或许我们可以这样说，真正令人满足的作品也必然对观者有所要求。[37]

建筑似乎能够以从道德层面影响人们的行为，这一论断当然要避免落入幼稚的决定论的陷阱。1951年，雅马萨基（纽约世贸中心的建筑设计师）为社会弱势群体设计了普鲁蒂·艾戈（Pruitt Igoe）住宅计划。这些建筑有11个楼层，总共有2870套公寓，其创新性备受瞩目，但楼房结构看起来容易引发故意破坏和犯罪行为，所以没有人愿意住在那里。这个建筑群在仅仅二十年后就被拆除了。

关于人们应如何生活以及开展哪些活动的特定理念会影响建筑的设计，而建筑物本身也会向其居住者倡导某些理念：一种显而易见的方式是让某些行动更便利，让其他行为更困难或者不可能开展。

"空间句法"的研究发现，不仅是出发点和目标之间的距离，还有城市的街道布局，都决定着人们选择的路线；人们更偏爱那些能提供视觉体验的道路［希利尔和利达，2005］。即使是人们的高度私密的决定，例如生育计划，似乎也受到居住条件的影响［瑞兹塔瑞科瓦和阿克曼，2003］。和普鲁蒂·艾戈项目一样，很多初衷良好的公共住宅项目结果却以失败告终。后来，建筑对人们心理的影响才成为了一个话题，并由此产生了一门新科学，即建筑心理学。[38] 建筑师及城市规划师

planner Oscar Newman (1935-2004) claimed that this is a general phenomenon: he had observed in a study in New York that high-rise apartment buildings occupied by many people show a higher crime rate than lower buildings, because their residents tended to show a greater personal responsibility for their place. Based upon this research, he developed the concept of "defensible space" suggesting a form of crime prevention (and increased public health) through community design.[39] Building design seems to discourage some kinds of behaviour and encourage others. Small, well-lit rooms with comfortable furniture, for example, can support social exchange in residential accommodation for old people. In 1957, the psychiatrist Humphry Osmond (1917-2004) labelled this quality "sociopetality" and characterised it as "that quality which encourages, fosters and even enforces the development of stable interpersonal relationships such as are found in small, face-to-face groups" ([Osmond, 1957], cited in [Lipman, 2003, p. 192]).

However, to what extent architectural forms are responsible (or even to be blamed) for the behaviour of the inhabitants remains controversial. The sociologist Alice Coleman, argues for a strong influence of urban structures [Coleman, 1985], but others have seen more important social factors at work that merely interact with the physical ones. Bill Hillier and others argued that many of Coleman's results were statistical artefacts and that the same forms might have been perfectly suitable for different inhabitants [Hillier, 1986].

But even if there were agreement on the factual question whether buildings can shape the life of people in such profound ways, there remains the questions of ideals and values: how do we evaluate any influence they may have on human behaviour? Again, it depends on the presupposed moral standards. If, for example, individual holism is seen as a moral ideal, as it is by Charles Taylor, then built environments which work against this should be criticized [Taylor, 1991, chapter 10]. More recent ideas of city planning, in favour of mixed uses rather then the zoning of different functions proposed in the 1933 Charter of Athens, seem a much more positive approach. However, "deconstructive" philosophers see a fragmented life as the authentic form of existence; and thus they should find nothing morally offensive in the alienating effect of a city which obeys the economic rules of the twenty-first century.

Two competing ideals of social life and behaviour are evident: an independent, autonomous life of the individual versus a community-oriented life. The first might be exemplified in Mies van der Rohe's designs of a series of court houses; while the interior of each is open-plan, they are all separated from each other by high garden walls. In contrast to this, the principles of "New Urbanism" are based upon the ideal of a strong community life where people should meet and interact. Independently from the concrete ideals that guide architecture in the fifth area, it is also questionable whether architecture should guide human behaviour at all. We might reject it morally because we think that architecture should also take our freedom and independence seriously. Thus architectural paternalism is especially to be avoided – but we should not be driven to the opposite but equally unacceptable response of simply providing unlimited choice. If, on the other hand, cities are built in accordance with abstract Utopian ideas like those of the Bauhaus, then architecture may fail because it is too demanding; it ignores what

奥斯卡•纽曼（1935-2004）认为这是个普遍现象：他在纽约的一项研究中注意到，居住人口众多的高层公寓楼比低层建筑物内发生的犯罪率要高，因为低层建筑物的住户往往对其住所展现出更高的个人责任感。在此项研究的基础上，他提出了"防御性空间"的概念，倡导一种通过社区设计来预防犯罪（并提升公众健康）的模式。[39] 建筑物的设计似乎能够阻止某些类型的行为，而鼓励另一些类型的行为。举例来说，光线充足、配有舒适家具的小型房间有利于老年人在其居所内开展社会交往。这一特性在1957年被心理医生汉弗莱•奥斯蒙德（1917-2004）定义为"社会向心环境"（sociopetality），其特点是 "它鼓励、推动甚至迫使人们形成稳定的人际关系，正如彼此面对面的小型群体里的关系那样"（[奥斯蒙德，1957]，引自 [利普曼，2003, p. 192]）。

然而，建筑形式要在多大程度上对居住者的行为负责（或是因此受到指责），这仍然是有争议的。社会学家爱丽思•科尔曼认为城市建筑有着强大的影响力[科尔曼，1985]，但在其他人看来，有更重要的社会因素在发挥作用，这些社会因素只是在与物理因素相互影响。比尔•希列尔等人表示，科尔曼的很多结论都是统计学结果，而且同样的形式可能完全适合于不同的居住者 [希利尔，1986]。

但是，即使人们就建筑物能否如此深刻地塑造我们的生活这一实际问题达成了一致，关于理想范式和价值观的种种问题仍然存在：我们要如何评估建筑物可能对人类行为造成的影响？在此再次强调，这取决于人们预先设定的道德标准。例如，如果像查尔斯•泰勒那样把个人的整体性视为一种道德理想，那么与之对立的建筑环境就应受到批评[泰勒，1991，第10章]。相较于1933年《雅典宪章》倡导的功能分区，近期的城市规划思想更偏爱混合使用，这一方式看起来更具积极意义。然而，在"解构主义"哲学家们看来，碎片式的生活是存在的本真形式；因此，面对一个按照21世纪经济规则建立的城市所带来的异化影响，他们应该不会在其中发现任何违背道德之处。

关于社会生活和行为，显然有两种对立的理念：一种是独立自主的个体生活，另一种是以社群为导向的生活。前者或许可以用密斯•凡•德罗设计的一系列法院建筑作为例证；尽管每栋建筑的内部都是开放式布局，但它们彼此之间都通过高高的花园围墙分隔开来。与此相反的是，"新城市主义"原则所立足的理念是强大的社区生活，人们应该见面和互动。建筑伦理的第五个领域里，除了那些对建筑起着指导作用的具体理念之外，关于建筑到底是否应该引导人们的行为，也是有异议的。我们可能从道德的角度排斥这种引导，因为我们认为建筑还应重视人们的自由和独立性。因此，尤其要避免建筑的包办家长式作风，但我们也不应转向其对立面，即提供过多的选择，这同样是不可接受的。另一方面，如果根据抽象的乌托邦式的观点——例如包豪斯学院的观点——来建造城市，那么建筑可能失败，因为要求过于苛刻；它无视人们的

people are capable of. A morally good architecture, it would seem, should take humans as they are, but should encourage them to grow beyond that.

6. Cultural or symbolic meaning

Not only the *architecture parlante* of the Revolutionary period in France, but architecture in general expresses something and thereby communicates ideas. Buildings can speak to us in a unique and powerful way and thus contribute to the process of arriving at new insights. "All architecture is a gesture", Wittgenstein writes, "Not every purposive movement of the human body is a gesture. And no more is every building designed for a purpose architecture" [Wittgenstein, 1980, p. 42]. Often the message of this "gesture" is about morally relevant themes. Buildings might encourage certain values in us, or might inspire us to overcome false ideals. Frank Lloyd Wright (1867-1959), for example, designed most of his so-called *Prairie Houses* around a fire-place or hearth that was pivotal, formally and symbolically, to the plan. This fire-place served not merely as physical gathering area, but served to express family life and its values, especially unity, harmony with nature and the simple life.

Architecture's functional nature has often been seen to oppose the idea of the building as an expressive artefact [Meyer, 1980, p. 34]. But why should it be impossible to "say something", that is to express an idea artistically, while realizing a given purpose? It seems that we can appreciate the aesthetic qualities of a house while (happily) living in it. Certainly, if the conditions within which the artefact is created do not leave any room for self-expression, where economic constraints ensure only a very limited range of forms for example, the criticism holds; not because something cannot be functional and an artwork in principle, but because in this instance the artisan has little or no freedom in the making of artistic choices. But to the extent that the creator is free, the (technical) craft turns into an art; and in most cases the creator will have some freedom. Even a clearly defined function can be realised in different forms. Great architects were able to understand the function of the building as a *theme* for their work that they "talked" about in the language of architecture. Brahms' *Requiem* and the *Taj Mahal* are both ingenious artworks that reflect upon death and its meaning for our life. To comprehend a work of art and its message is not merely a form (probably a deficient form) of intellectual insight (as rationalists like Baumgarten claimed); it is an experience *sui generis*, a unique form of becoming aware of something, which is different from rational understanding and from sensual pleasure. Since art can have a stronger motivational force than (by their nature abstract) logical arguments, art has a specific moral significance.

What, then, could be the morally relevant message of buildings *qua* art or artefact? Architectural messages can be morally relevant in many ways. In its symbolism a building can make us aware, for example, of the possibility of bridging between different cultures by exemplifying what Wolfgang Welsch has called "Transculturalism" [Welsch, 1996]. Buildings can also extol virtues or ideals – Bergilez and Genard have argued that the moral contribution of minimalist architecture is much needed today because this architecture expresses and promotes ideals such as "simplicité, dépouillement,

能力之所及。看来，从道德角度可称为善的建筑应接受人们本来的样子，但也应鼓励人们超越自身。

6. 文化或象征意义

不仅是法国革命时期的"会说话的建筑"，通常建筑都在表达一些东西，并由此传递思想。建筑物能够以一种独特而有力量的方式向我们说话，由此促进形成新的见解。"所有的建筑都有一种姿态"，维特根斯坦写道，"并非人身体的每一个有意识的活动都能形成一种姿态。同样地，并非每一栋建造物都能设计成为实现其意图的建筑"[维特根斯坦，1980，p. 42]。通常这种"姿态"的寓意都是与道德主题相关的。建筑物可能会激发起我们内在的某些价值观，或者激励我们纠正错误的思想。例如，弗兰克·劳埃德·赖特（1867-1959）设计的多数有"草原住宅"之称的房子，都围绕着一个壁炉或灶台，从形式和象征意义上，它都处于规划的中心位置。这个壁炉不只是供人们聚集的地方，更体现了家庭生活和价值观，尤其体现了团结、人与自然的和谐以及简单的生活。

人们常常以为，建筑的功能性与把它作为表达性的作品这一观点是相悖的［迈耶，1980，p. 34]。但是，为什么不能在实现既定用途的同时又"表达一些东西"，即在艺术上传递某种观点呢？我们是能够在一栋房屋里（开心）居住的同时也去欣赏它的美的例如经济条件的制约导致形式的选择范围极其有限；并不是因为从原则上有些东西不能兼具功能性和艺术性，而是因为在上述情况下，创作者在进行艺术选择的时候自由度很小或根本没有自由度。但是，只要创作者是自由的，（技术性）作品就可以转化为艺术；而且在绝大多数情况下，创作者都是享有一定自由度的。即使是一种被明确限定的功能，也可以用不同的形式予以实现。在那些伟大的建筑师看来，一栋建筑物的功能正是他们要用建筑语言去"探讨"的一个工作的主题。勃拉姆斯的《安魂曲》和泰姬陵都是精巧的艺术品，反思了死亡以及它对我们生活的意义。 人们了解一件艺术品及其传递的讯息，并不只是以（鲍姆加滕等理性主义者主张的）理智认知的方式（这很可能是一种不完善的方式）；它是一种独特的经验，是觉察到某些事物的一种独特方式，与理性认识以及感官享受是不同的。相比（本质上抽象的）逻辑论证，艺术有着更强大的感染力，所以它具有独特的道德意义。

那么，作为艺术或人工作品的建筑物传递的道德讯息又是什么呢？ 建筑传达的讯息在很多方面都可能与道德相关。例如，从象征意义上，一栋建筑通过彰显沃尔夫冈·韦尔施所说的"跨文化主义"[韦尔施，1996]，可以让我们意识到不同文化实现融合的可能性。建筑也可以颂扬美德或倡导理想——博尔吉勒兹和杰纳尔德指出，极简主义建筑在道德方面的贡献正是当今时代所急需的，因为这种建筑传达并倡导"simplicité, dépouillement, sérénité, intériorité" that can function as a critique of the omnipresent consumerist and economical worldview [Bergilez and Genard, 2004]. But whereas it is generally acknowledged that buildings should be safe and no threat to human health or life, and few would argue against the expectations for a green or sustainable architecture, there's little consent on whether there are cultural traditions that *should* (in a moral sense) be acknowledged in the architectural style of a region – and also, whether this is an ethical question at all, or merely an aesthetic choice.

It should be added that, first, it is obvious that to understand the message of a building some prior knowledge of the "language of architecture", as John Summerson has put it, is in most cases essential [Summerson, 1966]. That some knowledge is presupposed is not surprising, and, indeed, is the case throughout the arts. Secondly, the language—and thus meaning—of an architectural message can change over time; the meaning we attach to an artefact is inherently unstable. After all, meaning is neither simply created by the architect's intention nor by the physical features of the building; it is the way the community has reason to understand the artefact. Sometimes the changes of meaning over time can be dramatic. The *Cité de la Muette* near Paris was a public housing estate from the 1930s, but got transformed into a transit camp for jews during the German occupation. Later proposals to restore its housing function were rejected because of the meaning attached to it [Kroes and Primus, 2008]. Ceaucescu's palace in Bucharest provides an interesting case of a meaning which changed in the other direction, as it were. It is bigger than Versailles but not quite as big as the Pentagon, built at the end of a "Rajpath" longer and wider than New Delhi's, that was ruthlessly sliced through the fabric of the finest quarter of the old city. The destruction and vast building programme were carried out recklessly with record speed and efficiency. Surely this was a symbol of everything that is evil. But during the construction some 700 draughtsmen had been employed and countless craftspeople – in fact the construction, by using only Romanian materials, had encouraged a revivifying of craft traditions. And following the deposition of Ceaucescu parts of the huge building, named the "people's palace", have been hired out for weddings so that it is now regarded by some with pride and even affection.[40]

Ethics and ethos

Following the reflections by Heidegger on the right way of dwelling, Karsten Harries has argued for a more holistically "ethical" role of architecture. Humans are faced with a severe displacement in the modern world, Harries argues, that might be remedied by a renewed architecture. On a practical level, intimacy and belonging to a place are destroyed by modern technology like television, by which "the faraway and the nearby are equally brought into our living rooms, but only as pictures from which the observer is excluded" [Harries, 1975, p. 14]. But without distance, there is no intimacy, and without intimacy no place where one is at home: "When all places count the same we cannot place ourselves and become displaced persons". This displacement sérénité, intériorité"（简单、朴素、平静、内敛）的理念，能够对无所不在的消费主义和经济观形成批判 [博尔吉勒兹和杰纳尔德，2004]。可是，虽然人们公认建筑物应该是安全的，不应威胁到人们的健康或生活，也很少有人反对倡导绿色建筑或可持续性建筑，但是一个地区的建筑风格是否应当（从道德层面上）延续其文化传统，还有这究竟是一个伦理问题还是只不过是一种美学选择，人们对此并没有形成共识。

需要补充的是，首先，为了理解一栋建筑传递的讯息，如约翰·萨莫森所说，拥有一些"建筑学语言"的预设知识在多数情况下是至关重要的[萨莫森，1966]。有一些知识是预先设定好的，这并不奇怪，并且在整个艺术领域都是如此。其次，建筑讯息的语言——以及相应的含义——会随着时间而改变；我们赋予一项作品的意义从本质上说是不稳定的。毕竟，意义既不是简单地按照建筑师的意图创造的，也不是由一栋建筑的外型特征决定的；意义是人类社群运用理性去理解作品的途经。有些情况下，意义可能随着时间的流逝发生相当大的变化。巴黎附近的Cité de la Muette是二十世纪三十年代建成的公共住宅区，但在德军占领期间被改为犹太人集中营。因为其所承载的意义，后来关于恢复其住宅功能的提议都遭到了拒绝 [克洛斯和普里默斯，2008]。位于布加勒斯特的齐奥塞斯库的宅邸可以作为一个建筑意义发生方向性转变的有趣案例。这座宅邸比凡尔赛宫还大，但比五角大楼要小，建在一条比新德里国王大道更长更宽的 "国王大道"的尽头，这条大道无情地穿过一座古城最美好的区域。这个涉及拆毁以及大规模建造的项目是以创记录的速度和效率进行的。它固然是一切邪恶事物的象征。但是，在建造过程中它雇佣了大约700名制图员以及不计其数的工匠 ——事实上它的建造只使用了罗马尼亚材料，这促进了工艺传统的复兴。在齐奥塞斯库下台之后，这座被称为"人民宫"的巨大建筑局部被出租用于婚礼，所以现在有些人带着骄傲甚至是喜爱之情看待这座建筑。40

伦理和社会思潮

卡斯腾·哈里斯延续了海德格尔关于正确的栖居方式的反思，提出建筑承担着一种更为全面的 "伦理"角色。哈里斯指出，人类在现代世界里面临着严重的无处栖息的问题，重构建筑物可能会解决这一问题。在实际生活中，亲密感和对一个住所的归属感都受到了现代科技的破坏，以电视为例，它"把遥远世界和周围事物一同带入了我们的起居室，但这也只是一些把观者自己排除在外的画面罢了"[哈里斯，1975，p. 14]。然而，没有距离就没有亲密感，没有了亲密感，人就没有了家的感觉："如果所有的地方都是一样的，那么我们将无处栖息，从而变成流离失所的人。"无处栖息的问题

finds further support on a more theoretical level. Harries argues that the ideal of objectivity behind science and technology "transforms man from an embodied self into a pure thinking object", and is but another strong reason for the general displacement of humans. It is here that Harries hopes for a renewed architecture that creates an environment that will "give shape to our activities" so that we will be able to live a different life; it should bring individuals back to encounters with others and thus to a community life. This is, according to Harries, the most profound task of architecture: "To build is to help to decide how man is to dwell on the earth or indeed whether he is to dwell on it at all rather than drift aimlessly across it" [Harries, 1975, p. 15]. Harries calls this the Ethics of Architecture, because he sees it as closely connected to *ethos*, that is the characteristic mode of being of individuals and communities. Thus an ethical architecture is not supposed to follow moral rules or principles but to enable a new way of living individually and as a community with others; architecture should serve a common ethos.

Although this Ethics of Architecture claims to be different from (and not comparable with) more traditional approaches, it seems that this ideal of Ethics can be expressed in terms of the six areas above. Architecture assumes the task of opening our understanding and respect for nature and other humans (and our relationship to them) not merely on a discursive level, but rather by providing certain experiences. This admittedly holistic ideal includes mainly aspects of the fifth area (positive experience of a new possibility) and the sixth area (a better understanding of what it means to live and dwell).

Towards an Ethics of Architecture

An ethically satisfying architecture, it seems, would have to answer many different ethical demands, or at least offer a convincing trade-off. Building professionals often appear to have neglected most of these issues, or at least have not reflected upon them. And many architects see their profession as a branch of Aesthetics rather than ethics [Fisher, 2000], some even dismissing ethical demands altogether (as apologists for Post-modernism and Deconstructivism sometimes have done). And if there are good-willed ethical gestures, they are often perfunctory (such as the ubiquitous token references to "sustainability"), or are made from a political [Illies, 2005] or simplistically utilitarian perspective [Spector, 2001]. This is not to say that there are not architects who deal with green issues in a serious way – a general awareness is certainly growing.

Given its importance, it is surprising that moral philosophy has also paid almost no attention to the built environment. We find practical recommendations, mainly about "green" building, but no comprehensive ethical theory. That is not to say that ethical questions about architecture have not been frequently raised: the negative consequences of modern urban developments which were discussed by Lewis Mumford in the late 1930s, and the critique we have discussed from a phenomenological perspective illustrated by the work of Karsten Harries [1997]. Nevertheless, in 2000 Warwick Fox claimed that any Ethics of the built environment was "still in its infancy" [Fox, 2007].

在更为理论的层面上得到了进一步的论证。哈里斯指出，科学与技术背后的客观主义理念"把人从一个具有形体的自我变成了一个纯粹的思考的客体"，这是造成人类无处栖息的又一个重大原因。基于此，哈里斯希望有一个重构的建筑能创造一种环境去"塑造我们的活动"，从而让我们能过上一种不同的生活；它应该把人们带回到彼此相遇邂逅的环境中，从而重返社群生活。在哈里斯看来，建筑最重要的任务是："建造是为了帮助人们决定如何在地球上栖居，或者说人究竟是否要栖居在这里，而不是漫无目的地漂泊"[哈里斯，1975, p. 15]。哈里斯称其为建筑伦理学，因为他认为这与社会思潮紧密相关，这是个人和社群存在的特有模式。因此，一个伦理性的建筑并不是要遵循道德准则或原则，而是要带来一种新的个体生活方式以及与他人共处的社群生活方式；建筑应当为普遍的社会思潮服务。

尽管建筑伦理学声称它不同于以往传统的方式（且不具有可比性），这一伦理学思想似乎也可以用上文列举的六个领域来阐述。建筑承担的一项职责是展现我们对自然和对他人（以及我们与他人的关系）的理解与尊重，这不只是展现在论述层面，更要通过建筑提供的特定的体验来实现。这一公认的更为全面的思想涵盖了上文所列的第五个领域（对于一种新的可能性的积极体验）和第六个领域（对生存和栖居涵义的更深刻理解）的很多方面。

创建一门建筑伦理学

一个在伦理上令人满意的建筑看来必须满足很多不同的伦理要求，或者至少提供了一个有说服力的权衡方案。建筑界的专业人士似乎常常忽视了其中的绝大多数问题，或者说至少并未就这些问题进行反思。很多建筑师将其职业看做是美学的而不是伦理学的一个分支[费舍尔，2000]，有一些建筑师甚至完全不理会各种伦理要求（正如后现代主义和解构主义的辩护者有时候做的那样）。如果出现了一些善意的伦理姿态，通常也只是敷衍了事（例如那些随处可见的倡导"可持续性"的表面文章），或者是基于一种政治性的[伊利斯，2005]或单纯功利主义的视角[斯佩克特，2001]。这并不是说建筑师没有以一种严肃的方式对待环保问题——人们的环保意识当然是在不断增强的。

考虑到建筑环境的重要性，道德哲学竟然对这个议题几乎没有任何关注，这令人讶异。我们发现了一些主要与"绿色"建筑有关的实用建议，但没有找到任何全面的伦理理论。这并不是说人们没有频繁地提出建筑的伦理问题；刘易斯·芒福德在二十世纪三十年代末就探讨过现代城市发展带来的负面影响，我们也已经从现象学的角度讨论了卡斯腾·哈里斯[1997]作品展现出的批判性。尽管如此，瓦维克·福克斯在2000年声称，所有关于建筑环境的伦理学"仍处于发展初期"[福克斯，2007]。

In an account of "developments in the field of ethics of the built environment", Fox identified only ten philosophical contributions to such an Ethics [Fox, 2000, p. 3f]. Since then, however, the topic has been given more attention by philosophers as well as architects [Spector 2001; Ray, 2005b].

What are the reasons for this difficulty in developing an Ethics of the built environment? Besides the fact that many architects simply underestimate the problems and think that they can be solved with common sense, there are three principal reasons why it is so difficult: its inherent complexity, the difficulty of finding a clear definition, and an uncertainty about categories, particularly because of Ethics' intersection with Aesthetics.

The inherent complexity of architectural problems

As pointed out above, the built environment raises compound issues, because it is a highly complex activity, involving decisions, activities and reflections in very different areas that are governed by frequently heterogeneous requirements. The demand for sustainable architecture might, for example, clash with cultural values or the urgent need for cheaply available shelter. What is so special is architecture's inclusion of aesthetic issues and the balance required between demands of very different types: any architectural "answer" will have to balance aesthetic, technical, cultural, ecological, legal, political, and economical demands. This is something that can be found in very few other fields – even if they are also of high complexity like Medical Ethics.

Moreover, architecture has to provide a solution that works with the highest technical precision. Thus architects make judgements between unquantifiable and quantifiable goods, while being fully aware of the (often quantifiable) implications. This creates tensions that can grow into true dilemmas, because we do not have an obvious methodology as to how we should create a balance between them.[41] (And it is not even clear whether "balancing" is the right approach.)

The difficulty of finding a clear definition of architectural ethics

Although architecture raises so many problems, it is by no means clear whether there are problems so particular for architecture that they allow us to talk about a *specific* ethics. Many of architecture's moral challenges can be explored within the context of other ethics, for example environmental ethics (the second and partly the third of the issues raised above) or professional ethics (the first of those issues). We referred earlier to the problem of building for a TV station that contributes to a morally questionable government; it seems reasonable to apply here the *same* criteria for architects that we would apply for any businessman who thinks about a deal with a company. If that company is involved in severe violations of human rights, then one should not co-operate with it – unless there is reasonable hope that the engagement will improve the situation of those who suffer in some way.

What might be specific about an Ethics of Architecture? On the one hand, the clash

在梳理"建筑环境伦理学的发展"时，福克斯发现，关于这门伦理学只有十篇哲学稿件［福克斯，2000，p. 3f］。不过从那时起，哲学家和建筑师们都对这一主题给予了更多关注［斯佩克特，2001；雷，2005b］。

　　发展一门关于建筑环境的伦理学困难重重，是由哪些原因导致的？事实上很多建筑师对问题估计不足，并且认为这些问题用常识就可以解决，除此之外，还有三个重要原因使得建筑伦理学的发展很困难：它内在的复杂性；难以给它做出清晰的定义；以及范畴方面的不确定性，特别是它与美学是有交叉的。

建筑问题的内在复杂性

　　正如上文所指出的，建筑环境引发了复杂的问题，因为这是一项高度复杂的活动，涉及到在不同类型的要求的支配下在各个不同领域进行决策、活动和反思。举例而言，对于可持续性建筑的需求可能与文化价值或者对廉价容身之处的紧急需求之间存在冲突。建筑的特殊之处在于它涵盖了美学问题以及在各种不同类型的需求之间达到的平衡：任何一个建筑学"答案"都必须平衡美学、技术、文化、生态、法律、政治和经济层面的需求。这在其他领域——即使是医学伦理这种极其复杂的领域——都是很罕见的。

　　此外，建筑学必须提供一种技术精确度最高的解决方案。因此，建筑师要在不可量化的和可量化的对象之间做出判断，同时充分了解可能产生的（通常是可量化的）影响。由此引发的冲突有可能升级为真正让人进退两难的困境，因为并没有一种明确的方法告诉我们应该如何实现两者之间的平衡。[41]　（而且"平衡"本身是否就是正确的方式，也并不是很清楚。）

对建筑伦理学进行清晰定义所面临的困难

　　尽管围绕建筑提出了诸多问题，但这些问题是否是建筑特有的，以致于我们要探讨一门与它有关的特定的伦理学，这一点并不明确。建筑面临的很多道德挑战都可以在其他伦理学的范畴内进行探讨，例如环境伦理（上文提到的第二个问题，以及第三个问题的一部分）或者职业伦理（上文提到的第一个问题）。我们之前提到过为一个道德上有问题的政府建造电视台大楼的问题；这里我们对建筑师使用的标准与适用于那些计划和一家公司进行交易的商人们的标准是一样的，看来合情合理。如果该公司涉及严重违反人权的问题，那么人们就不应该与它合作，除非有合理的预期认定这一合作将在某种程度上改善受苦者的境遇。

between cultural sensitivity and economical constraints, between Aesthetics and green imperatives and the like cannot be classed merely under environmental or professional ethics. It is simply too complex – and this might be a good reason to ask for a specialised ethics for this area. On the other hand, we could focus on the problems that are specific for architecture. Fox finds it in:

> what we might call a building's 'design fit', that is, the extent to which a building fits with its natural, social, and built contexts when considered purely in terms of its design rather than in terms of its actual physical impact or even the preferences that people might have in regard to it. [Fox, 2008]

This comes close to suggesting that the uniqueness of Ethics applied to architecture lies in architecture giving in some way an *aesthetic* answer to complex moral problems. To be sure, that can also be asked from art if it is engaged in moral issues – but it will hardly ever reach the complexity of issues to be found in the built environment.[42]

The uncertainty about categories

Traditionally, ethics was focussed on human interactions, and it developed concepts, norms and values to be applied for this task. It is only recently (most obviously triggered through ecological and social problems) that ethics has turned systematically to new fields like technical artefacts.[43] As a consequence, traditional ethics is conceptually inadequate for buildings, cities, or the like.[44] Critics of the usage of "truth" in architecture (as employed by Ruskin in *The Seven Lamps of Architecture*, and before him Pugin) have pointed to the arbitrariness of the meaning given to "truth", and of the understanding that it can be achieved. As was pointed out in the introductory section, this also reveals a confusion between Aesthetics and ethics, one that continued into the twentieth century, when propagandists for Modernism claimed that the style was the only truthful expression of contemporary society and its technology. Decoration was therefore proscribed, and even the application of paint to a material like concrete was thought to devalue the quality of the material itself – ideally it should be left "fair-face" to express its character truthfully. It was for this reason that Reyner Banham's book on the "New Brutalism" from the 1950's was sub-titled "Ethic or Aesthetic?" [Banham, 1966].

So how shall we build? Although some values of an Ethics of Architecture seem particularly plausible, a normative theory is still needed that provides well justified ideals, values or goods for the different areas – and a theory that makes suggestions on how to deal with conflicting demands, both ethical and other, in specific cases. It is not clear yet what this theory might look like.

什么有可能是建筑伦理学所特有的呢？一方面，文化敏感度与经济条件制约之间的冲突、美学与环保责任之间的冲突等等，不能简单归入环境伦理或职业伦理的范畴。情况确实很复杂，这可能是建筑领域需要专门的伦理学的一个正当理由。另一方面，我们可以专注于建筑所特有的那些问题。福克斯指出：

> 我们所说的一栋建筑"设计得当"，即，一栋建筑在多大程度上契合了自然环境、社会环境和建筑背景，这里我们纯粹考虑其设计，而不考虑其实际影响或人们的偏好。[福克斯，2008]

这基本上说明，应用于建筑的伦理学其独特性在于，建筑从某种意义上对复杂的道德问题给出了一个美学的答案。当然，艺术领域在关注道德问题时也会产生类似的议题——但鲜少达到建筑环境所涉及的问题的复杂程度。[42]

关于分类的不确定性

在传统意义上，伦理学所关注的人际交往，伦理学发展出的概念、规范和价值观都是为了运用在这一方面。只是近年来（最明显的是受到生态问题和社会问题的影响），伦理学才开始系统性地转向技术产品等新的领域。[43] 因此，面对建筑、城市等等，传统伦理学从概念上是不充分的。[44] 批评家们指出，在建筑学中使用的"实相"概念（正如拉斯金在《建筑学七盏灯》中使用的，以及在他之前的皮金），人们所赋予它的含义以及对它的理解都存在着随意性。正如本章引言中指出的，这也揭示了美学和伦理学之间的混淆，这种混淆一直持续到二十世纪，此时现代主义的拥趸们声称，风格只是对当代社会及其技术的真实的呈现。因此装饰被禁止，甚至连在混凝土等材料上刷漆也被认为是降低了材料本身的品质，最理想的是保持"素颜"以真实表达其特点。正因如此，雷纳·班汉姆在二十世纪五十年代的著作《新野性主义》以 "伦理学还是美学？"作为副标题 [班汉姆，1966]。

那么我们应如何建造呢？尽管建筑伦理学的一些价值观看来十分合理，但我们仍然需要一种规范性理论，能够针对不同的领域提供合情合理的理念、价值观和产品，并且，关于在具体案例中如何应对伦理以及其他方面的彼此冲突的需求，这种理论也要能够提供建议。但是这种理论可能是什么样的，目前尚不清楚。

Aesthetics

We turn now to Aesthetics, a philosophical sub-discipline of prime importance for architecture. In an extraordinarily influential, but passing remark in De architectura, Vitruvius mentions "beauty" (venustas) as one of the three components of architecture, along with usefulness (utilitas) and technical integrity (firmitas) – and for almost 2000 years this triad has been the Leitmotiv of architectural theory and philosophical reflection on architecture [Vitruvius, 2001, Book 1]. Obviously, it has also played a major role for the practical building activity. Ever since antiquity, we find architectural beauty being aspired to – and admired: When he visited Babylon that had been re-erected by King Nebuchadnezzar II (c 630-562 BC), the historian Herodotus remarked that it "surpasses in splendour any city in the known world" [Herodotus, 1987, Book I, paragraph 178].

Yet although aesthetic values seem so important for architecture, there is little agreement about the theoretical or conceptual framework that might guide the building process aesthetically, or help to analyse architecture in aesthetic terms; the debate mirrors controversies that we find in all areas of philosophy. Moreover, architecture seems more difficult to grasp adequately than other artefacts. Building is a complex process in which many different people and skills are involved; the building's shape and form are determined by the architect(s), the craftsmen, the patron, and other stakeholders, but also by its place (the nature of its site) and urban context (neighbouring buildings); and this shape might change over time. What makes it even more complicated is that a building (unlike most paintings or pieces of music) is fulfilling a certain function and having some utility. As Roger Scruton remarks: "Hence, although we may have reason to think that we sometimes treat buildings as aesthetic objects, it does not follow that in appreciating them as buildings we are appreciating them aesthetically" [Scruton, 1979].

In what follows, we will approach the aesthetic aspect of architecture by looking at different alternatives and debates that can be found in the tradition. The first will be in relation to theory; there is a fundamental difference in whether we take Aesthetics to be about some objective values that can be discovered in a rational process or whether it is about subjective responses to certain sensual experiences. After that, we turn to the search for key concepts or categories for the aesthetic appreciation of architecture: here the 18th century debate on the sublime, the beautiful and the picturesque will serve as an example, but we will also talk about empathy. Thirdly, we turn briefly to the central problem of Aesthetics and utility that we have just mentioned: is architecture capable of being judged aesthetically at all? Fourthly, we will link some of the considerations with the ethical debate above: Aesthetics is not merely in potential conflict with functional

美学

现在我们转向美学，这是一个对于建筑至关重要的哲学子学科。在《建筑十书》一篇非常有影响力但又很随意的评论中，维特鲁威提到"美"（venustas）时，将其作为建筑的三个组成部分之一，另外两个是"实用"（utilitas）和"坚固"（fimitas）。近 2000 年来，这个三元体一直是建筑理论和建筑哲学思维的主导[维特鲁威，2001 年，第 1 册]。它对于实际的建筑活动显然也起了重要作用。自那时起，我们发现建筑美一直被人们所追求——而且被赞美：当历史学家希罗多德（Herodotus）访问由尼布甲尼撒二世（King Nebuchadnezzar II）（公元前 630－562年）重建的巴比伦时，他评论说："它的辉煌壮丽超过了已知世界中的任何城市"（希罗多德，1987 年，第一卷，第 178 段）。

然而，尽管美学价值对于建筑来说显得如此重要，但是人们在理论或概念性框架方面鲜有一致意见，理论或框架可以从美学的角度指导建筑过程，或帮助人们用美学术语去分析建筑；这场辩论中反映出的诸多争议，我们在所有的哲学领域里都能看到。此外，相对于其他人工作品来说，建筑似乎更难被人们充分理解。建筑是一个复杂的过程，其中涉及许多不同的人员和技能；建筑的形状和形式不仅由建筑师、工匠、雇主和其他利益相关者决定，而且由其选址（场所的性质）和城市环境（周遭建筑）决定；而它的形状可能随着时间的推移而发生改变。更加复杂的地方在于，一栋建筑（不同于绝大多数绘画或音乐作品）需要实现一个特定的功能，具备一些功用。正如罗杰·斯克鲁顿（Roger Scruton）所说的那样："所以，虽然我们可能有理由认为在某些时候可以将建筑物当作美学的对象去看待，但我并不意味着当我们将它们作为建筑物来欣赏时，我们是在从美学的角度去欣赏。"（斯克鲁顿（Scruton），1979 年）。

接下来，我们将通过考察存在于传统中的不同的方式和争论，来探讨建筑的美学层面。首先是理论方面。我们是将美学理解为在理性过程中发现的一些客观价值，还是将美学看做是对特定感性体验做出的主观反应，这两者之间有着重大的差别。其次，我们转向寻找建筑美学欣赏的那些关键概念或类别：这里以十八世纪关于崇高、优美和如画美的辩论为例，但我们也会谈及移情。第三，我们简单探讨了刚刚提到的关于美学和实用性的核心问题——美学和效用：建筑能够完全用美学来评判吗？第四，我们将把一些思考与前文的伦理学讨论联系起来：美学不仅与功能层面的

demands but also with moral demands (amongst others). The complex nature of architecture, namely that it should satisfy different and often heterogeneous requirements at the same time, is mirrored in tensions that go beyond the classic form versus function dichotomy. We will conclude this section, fifthly, by making a constructive suggestion about different types of beauty that can and should be applied to buildings.

The problem of theory

The empiricist philosophy of art and beauty is most evident with British philosophers like Shaftesbury, Hutcheson, Hume and Burke. Empiricist Aesthetics sees aesthetic judgements fundamentally as expressions of subjective states of mind or feelings that are shaped and conditioned by experiences, culture, or other contingent causes. It denies that beauty is a quality inherent in some object. Certainly a subjective response is still seen as a *reaction* to certain formal features of the object, but that response is something over and above a mere perception of its properties. Thus, for subjectivism, the idea of universal rules or standards is pointless. The popular version of aesthetic subjectivism is the wide-spread view that *de gustibus non est disputandum* – we cannot, and indeed should not argue about matters of taste: they are personal. But we are all aware that the process of development control, whereby planning committees are advised by panels of experts and come to conclusions as to what buildings are to be approved and what are to be prevented, involves (or at least should involve) aesthetic judgements about the buildings under consideration. And there is naturally plenty of dispute.

In contrast to the empirical approach, there is a (Continental) rationalist or cognitive Aesthetics. Alexander Gottlieb Baumgarten (1714-1762), one of the founding fathers of Aesthetics as a discipline, defined Aesthetics as the "science" of sensory cognition [Baumgarten, 1750, § 1]. Although he subscribed to a different understanding of Aesthetics (in which he included *all* sense of perception) than our own would be, he initiated a pursuit for a rationalist Aesthetics that would aim at universal insights and general rules. For Baumgarten and the continental tradition, in particular Immanuel Kant, "beauty" is not to be understood in terms of a physiological process or merely by means of a subjective response but has more to do with rational ideas, and objective standards.

But what might these standards be? We have seen that within architecture, Leon Battista Alberti presupposed a cognitive aesthetic when he claimed that beauty was mainly a matter of the right *proportion* – that is the relationship of parts to a whole and to one another. "In all perfectly beautiful objects there is found the opposition of one part to another and a reciprocal balance", as John Ruskin puts it more poetically [Ruskin, 1878-79]. And since Greek antiquity, the Golden Ratio,[45] especially in form of the Golden Rectangle, has been considered as an objective standard providing the right balance for the formal composition of Western architecture.[46] This ratio was seen as derived from the (idealised) human body, as the mathematician Pythagoras (560-480 BC) had already tried to show.[47]

要求存在潜在的冲突，而且与道德层面的要求（以及其他要求）也存在潜在的冲突。建筑的复杂性——即它需要同时满足各种不同的而且往往是类别迥异的要求——在诸多冲突中反映出来，不止是形式与功能之间的经典的二元论冲突。第五，不同类型的美可以而且应该运用到建筑当中，我们对此提出了一条建设性的建议，以此结束本章的讨论。

理论问题

关于艺术和美的经验主义哲学，在英国哲学家（如沙夫茨伯里（Shaftesbury），哈里奇（Hutcheson），休谟（Hume）和伯克（Burke））那里表现得最为明显。经验主义美学认为，审美判断从根本上说是主观心理状态或感情的表达，而这种心理状态或感情是由经验、文化或其他偶然因素所塑造和制约的。它否认美是某个客体所固有的品质。当然，主观反应仍然被看作是对客体的某些形式特征所作出的回应，但是这种回应超越了对客体属性的单纯的感知。因此，对于主观主义而言，那些关于普遍规则普遍标准的想法是毫无意义的。美学主观主义的流行版本持这样一种广泛流传的观点：品味无可争辩——我们不能，而且事实上也不应该就品味之事进行争辩：品味是个人的事情。但是我们都知道，在开发管制的过程中，规划委员会在专家小组的建议下关于批准哪些建筑和禁止哪些建筑得出结论，这个过程就涉及到（或至少应该涉及）对所考察的建筑物的美学判断。这个过程中当然有很多争论。

与经验的方式相反，还有一种（欧洲大陆的）理性主义美学或认知美学。亚历山大·戈特利布·鲍姆加滕（Alexander Gottlieb Baumgarten）（1714—1762年）——将美学设为一门学科的创始人之一——将美学定义为感官认知的"科学"（鲍姆加滕，1750年，§1）。尽管他对美学的理解（其中他囊括了所有的感官认知）与我们的理解不同，但是他发起了对一种理性美学的追寻，这种美学旨在探寻普遍见解和一般规则。对于鲍姆加滕和大陆传统特别是伊曼努尔·康德（Immanuel Kant）而言，对"美"的领略并不是依照心理过程或仅仅依靠主观反应而获得的，而是更多地涉及到理性思想和客观标准。

但是这些标准可能是什么呢？我们已经知道，在建筑学当中，当莱昂·巴蒂斯塔·阿尔伯蒂宣称美学主要是关于正确比例——即部分与整体和各部分之间的关系——的问题时，他预先假设了一种认知美学。约翰·拉斯金（John Ruskin）的表述更为诗意一些："在所有完全美丽的客体中，都可以发现一个部分与另一个部分的对立和相互平衡。"（拉斯金，1878—1879年）自古希腊以来，黄金分割率[45]——特别是黄金矩形形式的黄金分割率——一直被认为是使西方建筑的形式构造获得良好平衡的一个客观标准。[46] 这个比率被认为是来源于（理想化的）人体，数学家毕达哥拉斯（Pythagoras，公元前560—480年）曾经试图证明这一点。[47]

The main argument in favour of aesthetic subjectivism is the different conceptions of beauty, both within a culture and between different cultures. In answer, cognitivists point to the surprising agreement about what are architectural masterpieces in very different cultures – the Taj Mahal or Chartres Cathedral are almost universally praised.[48] Notably, even the empiricist David Hume wrote that taste is "far fewer liable to the revolutions of chance and fashion than these pretended decisions of science" [Hume, 1757, paragraph 26]. Further, cognitivists reason that we can, after all, *argue* successfully about the qualities of artworks, for example *why* Elgar's Enigma Variations or Mies van der Rohe's Pavilion in Barcelona are – or should be – admired by musicians or architects. Such rational discussion seems only comprehensible if we presuppose that there are some (minimal) standards as common points of reference.

There are also attempts to find a middle ground between a strict cognitivist Aesthetics and an understanding of Aesthetics as being about subjective responses, for example pragmatist approaches. In his architectural Aesthetics, Julian Roberts uses the analogy of British case law (rather than Roman Law), and argues that aesthetic judgment, though it should be informed, would more properly be like a "trial by jury" than an oracular judgment issued by persons with a special training [Roberts, 2005]. The historian Peter Collins, tends to agree, distinguishing between principles and laws and quoting a famous case from 1761 (Hamilton *versus* Meades) that negotiations should depend on rules that are the result of "the dictates of common sense drawn from the truth of the case" [Collins, 1971]. Although pragmatic approaches have been of major importance in architectural practice (many aesthetic decisions in urban planning are made by commissions of lay-people), it might be objected that they face the conceptual difficulties of many other "bottom-up" approaches.[49]

Key concepts for the aesthetic appreciation of architecture

What are the basic categories for an Aesthetics of architecture? An important examination of how people might be affected by architecture (and by natural landscape) was undertaken in eighteenth century England, just at the time that Aesthetics was born as a philosophical discipline. One of the most influential theorists was Edmund Burke, the author of *A Philosophical Enquiry into the Origin of our Idea of the Sublime and the Beautiful*, written in 1757-59. As his title suggests, Burke aimed to distinguish between two qualities that we might appreciate aesthetically.

In the *Enquiry*, this is how Burke defines the *sublime*:

> whatever is fitted in any sort to excite the ideas of pain and danger, that is to say whatever is any sort terrible, or is conversant about terrible objects, or operates in a manner analogous to terror, is in a sense sublime; that is it is productive of the strongest emotion which the mind is capable of feeling. I say the strongest emotion, because I am satisfied the ideas of pain are much more powerful than those which enter on the part of pleasure. [Burke, 1759, Part I, Section VII, p. 36]

支持美学主观主义的主要论据是美的不同概念，这些不同的概念既存在于一种文化内部，也存在于不同的文化之间。作为回应，认知主义者们指出，在截然不同的文化里，关于什么是建筑杰作，答案竟出奇地一致——泰姬陵或沙特尔大教堂几乎获得了普遍的赞誉。[48] 值得注意的是，就连经验主义者大卫·休谟（David Hume）也曾经写道，品味"与那些伪装的科学决定相比，受到机遇和风尚变革的影响要小得多"（休谟，1757 年，第 26 段）。此外，认知主义者们认为，我们毕竟可以对艺术作品的质量成功地进行辩论，例如埃尔加（Elgar）的谜语变奏曲或密斯·凡·德罗（Mies van der Rohe）的巴塞罗那展馆为什么受到——或应该受到——音乐家们或建筑师们的称赞。看来只有当我们预先假设有某些（最低限度的）标准作为共同的参考，这种理性讨论才是可以理解的。

还有人试图在严格的认知主义美学与将美学视为主观反应的观点之间找到一个中间立场，例如实用主义的方法。朱利安·罗伯茨（Julian Roberts）在其建筑美学中，以英国判例法（而不是罗马法）作为类比，认为美学判断虽然应该了解情况，但是它的确更像是"陪审团的审判"而不是由受过特殊训练的人们作出的审判判决[罗伯茨，2005 年]。历史学家彼得·柯林斯（Peter Collins）将原则和法律区分开来，并引用了 1761 年的一个著名案例（汉密尔顿诉米纳斯），倾向于认为协商应以规则为基础，而这些规则就是"根据案件真相凭常识得出的"结果（柯林斯，1971 年）。尽管实用主义的方式在建筑实践中一直具有重要的意义（城市规划中的许多美学决定是由人民委员会作出的），但是这也可能招来反对，认为这些方法和许多其他"自下而上"的方法一样，面临着概念上的难题。[49]

建筑美学欣赏的一些关键概念

建筑美学的基本类别是什么？在十八世纪，恰逢美学作为一个哲学学科诞生之时，英格兰进行了一次关于人们如何被建筑（和自然景观）影响的重要调查。最有影响的理论家之一是埃德蒙·伯克（Edmund Burke），他著有《关于崇高和优美的概念起源的哲学探究》（A Philosophical Enquiry into the Origin of our Idea of the Sublime and the Beautiful），该书写于 1757—1759 年。正如书名所示，伯克旨在将我们从美学的角度欣赏的两种品质区分开来。

在《探究》一书中，伯克是这样定义崇高的：

> 凡是以某种方式引发了痛苦的和危险的想法，即，任何事物凡是能以某种方式引起恐惧，或者与恐怖的对象关系密切，又或以类似于恐怖的方式运转着，这些事物在某种意义上就是崇高的；也就是说，它可以引发心灵能够感觉到的最强烈的情感。我说最强烈的情感，因为痛苦的想法远比那些沉入乐趣之中的想法更为强烈，这令我很满意。[伯克，1759 年，第一部分，第七节，第 36 段]

In moving on to describe *beauty*, Burke turns to the question of sexual reproduction to illustrate how, in the act of love, in humans, a brute animal passion is replaced by "a mixed passion which we call love", and the object of this mixed passion is beauty [Burke, 1759, Part I, Section X, p. 39]. We must expect to find combinations of the qualities of the sublime and the beautiful in every work of art, but Burke avoids the naming of any third intermediate term – he is content to describe differences [Burke, 1759, part III, Section XXVII, pp. 113-114]. The aesthetic distinctions which Burke draws between the sublime (huge, rough, awesome, natural, overwhelming) and the beautiful (petite, smooth, highly fashioned and seductive) can be read psychoanalytically, economically and politically, and, since Part V is concerned with words, the *Enquiry* has also proved fertile ground for twentieth century scholars concerned with rhetoric and the workings of language itself.[50]

The appreciation of some contemporary architectural work (such as Rem Koolhaas' "Large" and "Extra-Large" buildings, discussed below) would fall into the category of the sublime: we would be moved and awed by their scale, and maybe enjoy the pain of their brutal acceptance of the given conditions. The enjoyment of beauty becomes a private matter, confined to the erotics of the bedroom, since the condition of Modernism is such that an un-mediated, un-ironic public enjoyment of beauty is no longer possible.

Later in the eighteenth century, writers sought the middle term that Burke avoided, which would combine elements of the sublime and the beautiful. William Gilpin's *Three Essays: On Picturesque Beauty; on Picturesque travel; and On Sketching Landscape*, published in 1792, and Uvedale Price's *"Essays on the Picturesque as compared with the Sublime and the Beautiful"* of 1810 both advocate the concept of the picturesque. The picturesque shares with the sublime something of its roughness. And it "may be great or small" writes Gilpin, "but since it so depends on the character of boundaries, can never be infinite". In other words the picturesque is always framed. The symmetry and perfection of the Beautiful must be defaced in order for it to become picturesque. Gilpin recommends taking a mallet to Tintern Abbey: "we must beat down one half of it, deface the other, and throw the mutilated members around in heaps" [Gilpin, 1792; cited in Punter, 1994, p. 235].[51] The picturesque does not, therefore, participate in the dangerously erotic character of the beautiful: the figure in a picturesque landscape is more likely to be a decrepit hag than a young woman. "In real life, I fancy", wrote Price, "the most picturesque old woman, however her admirer may ogle her on that account, is perfectly safe from his caresses" [Price, 1842].

The picturesque is in fact a melancholic view of beauty – the pleasure of ruins lying both in the satisfying effect to the eye of their composition and the sense that they communicate of their being fragments of an ideal world that we can no longer achieve. There are several examples of nineteenth-century architects who anticipated the decay of their buildings in the way in which they represented them. One such would be John Soane, whose proposals for the Bank of England were illustrated in ruins before they were even constructed. He was a friend of the artist Henri Fuseli, who shared his deep pessimism

接着在描述美时，伯克转向了性繁殖的问题，来说明在人类爱的行为里，一种野兽动物式的激情如何被"我们称之为爱的一种混杂的激情"所替代，这种混杂的激情的对象就是美[伯克，1759 年，第一部分，第十节，第 39 段]。我们必然期待着在每一件艺术作品中找到崇高和优美的品质的结合，但是伯克避而不用任何第三个术语去命名这个中间状态——他满足于描述崇高和优美之间的差异[伯克，1759 年，第三部分，第二十七节，第 113–114 段]。伯克在崇高（巨大的、粗糙的、可怕的、自然的、压倒性的）与优美（娇小的、光滑的、深度加工过的和诱人的）之间所做的美学区分，可以从精神分析、经济和政治的角度来解读，由于书的第五部分与词语有关，《探究》一书也被证明是二十世纪关注修辞和关注语言自身发展的学者们的一片沃土。[50]

对一些当代建筑作品（如雷姆·库哈斯（Rem Koolhaas）的"大型"和"超大型"建筑，下面将讨论）的欣赏，可以归入崇高一类：我们会被它们的规模所感动和震撼，并且也许会享受它们直面既定环境而产生的痛苦。对美的享受变成了一件私事，局限于卧室的情色，因为现代主义的环境是这样的：无需中介、不带讽刺地公开享受美，已经变得不可能了。

后来在十八世纪，作家们纷纷寻求伯克所回避的中间术语，它结合了崇高和优美的元素。威廉·吉尔平（William Gilpin）于 1792 年出版的《三篇文章：关于如画美；关于如画的旅行；以及关于写生风景》（Three Essays: On Picturesque Beauty; on Picturesque travel; and On Sketching Landscape），和尤夫德尔·普赖斯（Uvedale Price）于 1810 年出版的《与崇高和优美相对照的如画美随笔》（Essays on the Picturesque as compared with the Sublime and the Beautiful），都倡导如画美的概念。如画美与崇高都具有粗糙的特点。"如画美可能场面很大或很小，"吉尔平写道，"但是由于它对边界的特点如此依赖，因此永远不可能是无限的。"换句话说，如画美始终是有框架的。为了成就如画美，优美的对称性和完美性必须被毁坏。吉尔平建议带一个槌子到丁登寺（Tintern Abbey）："我们必须将它的一半打倒，将另一半丑化，把残破的各部分随处堆放。"[吉尔平，1792 年；引用于《赌博者》（Punter），1994 年，第 235 页]。[51] 因此，如画美不具备优美那种可能引发危险的情色的特征：如画景致之中的人物更像是一个垂垂老妪，而不是一位年轻女郎。普赖斯写道："我想，在现实生活中，一个如画的老女人，无论怎样被她的爱慕者定睛凝视，她都是十分安全的，不会被他爱抚。"[普赖斯，1842 年]

如画美实际上是关于美的一个忧郁的视角——废墟带给人的愉悦既在于其构造取悦了我们的眼睛，也在于它所传达的感觉，即这些废墟是我们再也不能实现的理想世界的碎片。以几个十九世纪建筑师为例，他们期待其建筑作品以他们所描绘的方式衰败下去。其中一位是约翰·索恩（John Soane），他关于英格兰银行的草案是用废墟来呈现的，哪怕当时还尚未建造。他是画家亨利·富塞利（Henri Fuseli）的朋友，富塞利和索恩一样，都对当下的艺术水平

69

about the state of the arts, which he regarded as debased in comparison to the vision of antiquity held by Winckelmann and Flaxman. Fuseli's position, and thus we may infer Soane's, is summed up in his famous etching of 1778-9 *The Artist moved by the grandeur of ancient ruins*, a poignant evocation of his melancholic attitude to the past. And this attitude survives into the twentieth century. Alvar Aalto, whose Baker House is considered below, avoided symmetry in his buildings, and frequently seems to suggest fragmentary ruins in the vicinity of his own work (notably in his summer house at Muuratsalo). He also evokes an ancient precedent by representing an outdoor amphitheatre in the landscape at the Jutland art gallery, and at his own office at Tiilimäki, which is eroded at its edges as if it has been there for many centuries.

How we view architecture need not be mediated by eighteenth century theory, however, and might be understood at a more profound, psychological, level. Firstly, our appreciation of architecture is not merely visual. The historian Heinrich Wölfflin has already been mentioned. His 1886 *Prolegomena to a Psychology of Architecture* refers to Goethe's remark that "we ought to sense the effect of a beautiful room, even if we were led through it blindfolded" in his argument that "the architectural impression, far from being some kind of "reckoning by the eye", is essentially based on direct bodily feeling."[52] Architecture is not just a visual art, but something we "feel" with all our senses. Arguments about style often use linguistic analogies – architecture is a language which is "spoken" grammatically or practised illiterately; the syntactically uneducated "vernacular" is compared to the sophisticated grammatical work of educated architects – but as an experience architecture is actually more primitive and basic. Perhaps the first "architectural" experience is that of birth – a passage from dark to light, from enclosed and protected to open and unprotected, from within the comfort of the womb to the exposure to the world. The remark by the literary critic Cyril Connolly that architecture was a "womb with a view" was not only a witty reference to a novel by E.M. Forster, but refers to the distinction of experience that we all may have as children when we construct our first shelters. We make a "tree house" up in the branches, and hollow out a cave between its roots. Of the great psychoanalysts in the twentieth century, Freud was comparatively uninterested in architecture, though his pupil Melanie Klein affected art historical theory through her erstwhile patient Adrian Stokes. Stokes' descriptions of the distinction between "carved" and "modelled" forms relate psychoanalytical mental states to the way in which sculpture and architecture is fashioned. The complex (some would say muddled) but influential thinking of Carl Jung is a more common underpinning to the way in which people often express their feelings about buildings. Jung conceived a theory of archetypes – typical images and their associations that transcend cultural boundaries – and some have tried to relate what we find pleasing in buildings (or in city environments) to those archetypes.[53] There is an element of Platonic idealism in Jung's notion, since it would imply that satisfactory architectural images referred back to some archetypal form which is inherently satisfying on an instinctual level.

If aesthetic appreciation goes beyond the visual, perhaps it is more empathetic. At its most basic, an empathetic theory of architectural understanding implies that, on the

持深刻的悲观情绪；富塞利认为，与温克尔曼（Winckelmann）和弗拉克斯曼（Flaxman）持有的古代视角相比，艺术水平变低了。富塞利的立场——据此我们也可以推断出索恩的立场——在其 1778-1779 年著名的蚀刻作品《被古代废墟之宏伟壮丽所感动的艺术家》（The Artist moved by the grandeur of ancient ruins）中做了典型概括，这部作品深刻地呈现了他对于过去的忧郁态度。这种态度持续到了二十世纪。阿尔瓦·阿尔托（Alvar Aalto）——其贝克楼将在下文讨论——在其建筑中避免了对称性，并且似乎经常建议在其作品附近（其中比较突出的是在穆拉特萨的夏季房屋）设置碎片废墟。他还通过在日德兰半岛艺术画廊和自己位于提里马基（Tiilimäki）的办公室周围景观当中设计一个圆形剧场，重现一个古老的先例，剧场的边沿被侵蚀，仿佛已经存在了许多世纪。

　　关于我们应如何观赏建筑，其实并不需要被十八世纪的理论所引导，而或许可以从更为深刻的心理的层面去理解。首先，我们对建筑的欣赏不仅仅是视觉上的欣赏。历史学家海因里希·沃尔夫林（Heinrich Wölfflin）已经在前文中被提到了。在他 1886 年的《建筑心理学导论》（Prolegomena to a Psychology of Architecture）中，在论证"建筑的印象远不是某种'眼睛的推断'，而是本质上基于直接的身体感觉"时，他引用了哥德的观点，即"我们应该感受一个美丽房间的效果，即使我们被蒙住眼睛带进房间"。[32]建筑不仅仅是一种视觉艺术，而是我们用所有感官"感受"到的东西。关于风格的争论当中经常用修辞学做类比——建筑是一种语言，或是按语法去"讲述"，或是在纯朴地表达；句法上未受教育熏陶的"白话"，被比作是受过教育的建筑师的高级的语法作品——不过建筑作为人们的一种经验，其实更为原始和基本。也许第一个"建筑的"经验像是出生那样——是一个从黑暗到光明、从封闭和受保护到开放和不受保护、从子宫内的舒适到暴露于世界的过程。文学评论家西里尔·康诺利（Cyril Connolly）说建筑是一个"带有视野的子宫"，这不仅机智引用了 E. M. 福斯特（E. M. Forster）的一部小说，而且涉及到了可能所有人都有过的在孩提时代建造我们的第一个庇护所这一经历具有的特质。我们在树枝上造一个"树屋"，在其根部之间挖出一个洞穴。在二十世纪伟大的精神分析学家们之中，相对来说弗洛伊德（Freud）对建筑学不感兴趣，虽然他的学生梅兰妮·克莱（Melanie Klein）通过她以前的病人艾德里安·斯托克斯（Adrian Strokes）而影响了艺术史理论。斯托克斯在描述"雕刻"和"建模"形式之间的区别时，将精神分析学的心理状态与雕塑和建筑的塑造方式联系起来。卡尔·荣格（Carl Jung）那复杂（有些人会说是混乱）但颇具影响力的思维，对于人们经常表达对建筑的感觉时所采用的方式提供了一种更为普遍的支持。荣格构思出了原型——即典型的图像及其超越文化边界的关联性——的理论，有些人已经尝试着将我们在建筑物（或城市环境）中发现的令人愉悦的东西与这些原型联系起来。[53]在荣格的观念中有一种柏拉图式唯心主义的元素，因为它暗示道，令人满意的建筑图像要回溯到某个原型形式，该原型形式本身从直觉上就是令人满意的。

　　如果超越了视觉的层面，美学鉴赏或许更具有移情的效果。关于建筑理解的移情理论从最基本的层面上指出，类似于

analogy of an empathy with other people, in perceiving a building we both imagine ourselves inhabiting the spaces, and in some way put ourselves in the place of the elements of the construction. In everyday practice, architects might be expected to exercise empathy – to imagine themselves in the situation for which they are designing (Aalto claimed that his Paimio sanatorium design was influenced by his own experience in hospital when he was forced to gaze at the ceiling for a long period of time), but the real issue is how someone who experiences the building can be expected to exercise empathy. One of the characteristics of the classical orders was that they were characterised by gender: Doric was the sturdiest and most masculine, Ionic was feminine, as was Corinthian – but a more attenuated and graceful representation of the gender. Sometimes the Doric order could be substituted by statues – these are Atlantids. And taking the place of the Corinthian order, most famously in the Erechtheum in Athens, would be Caryatids. In aesthetic thinking the idea is associated with Theodor Lipps and Robert Vischer, who coined the term *Einfühlung* ("in-feeling" or "feeling-into") in his 1873 doctoral thesis.[54] In perceiving a building we therefore expect the strongest part of the composition to be where the heaviest loads are taken, nearest the ground. The use of "rustication" in classical architecture responds to that expectation, just as pilasters attached to a masonry wall dramatise the pattern of load as well as "ordering" the façade dimensionally. Modern Architecture, which rejoices in dramatic cantilevers and tends to have slender columns (or *piloti*) at ground level arguably achieves much of its aesthetic effect precisely because it subverts those expectations.

Aesthetics and utility

As mentioned above, it has sometimes been argued that architecture should be seen as primarily functional – utility (*utilitas*) being, besides firmness (*firmitas*), another of the three basic qualities that Vitruvius introduces. Firmness refers to it being solid and lasting, while utility means the function of the building (e.g. a temple) and its general usefulness of providing protection for its users etc. For Vitruvius, and classic philosophy in general, this triad would be seen as a unity; the good and the beautiful seemed necessarily linked or at least their harmony the ideal to strive for. (Thus the ideal man was seen as having moral and aesthetic qualities, he was handsome *and* brave – *Kalos kai agathos*, as the tradition since Herodotus called it). This ideal of harmony still guides Alberti in his already quoted definition of beauty: "that reasoned harmony of all the parts within a body, so that nothing may be added, taken away, or altered, but for the worse" [Alberti, 1998].

But in the influential teaching of the Bauhaus, at least at some stages, function was accorded the primary role. The director during the period between 1928 and 1930, Hannes Meyer (1889-1954), wrote that:

> Building is a technical, not an aesthetic process, and time and again the artistic composition of a house has contradicted its practical function. Planned in ideal and basic terms, our house will become a piece of machinery.[55]

对他人产生的移情作用，在感知一个建筑时，我们既想像自己居住在其空间内，又以某种方式将自己置身于建设元素的位置。在日常实践中，人们可能期待建筑师们进行移情——建筑师想像自己处于所设计的环境之中（阿尔托声称，他的帕伊米奥疗养院设计受到了他自己在医院的经历的影响，当时他被迫长时间盯着天花板），但真正的问题是，体验建筑的人们如何能够按照期望的那样进行移情。古典柱式的特征之一是它们的性别特征：多立克柱式是极为坚固和极具男性特征的，爱奥尼亚柱式则具有女性特征，科林斯柱式也是女性化的——但其性别呈现更为纤细，也更为优雅。有时，多立克柱式可以被雕像替代，这些雕像就是亚特兰蒂斯。而代替科林斯柱式的则是女骑士，最著名的是在雅典的厄瑞克修姆庙中。在美学思维中，移情的理念与西奥多·利普斯（Theodor Lipps）和罗伯特·维切尔（Robert Vischer）有关，罗伯特在其 1873 年的博士论文中创造了"Einfühlung"（"内情感"或"深刻感受"）这个词。[54] 在感知建筑物时，我们因此而期望该组合物最坚固的部分是承载最重负荷、最接近地面的地方。古典建筑中使用的"锈蚀"是对人们这种期望的回应，正如与砌体墙联结的壁柱，生动展现了负荷的形象，并从空间上对建筑物的正面做了"安排"。现代建筑——其戏剧性的悬臂，偏好在地面上设置细长的柱子——可以说很好地实现了它的美学效果，恰恰因为它颠覆了这些期望。

美学与实用性

如上所述，有时人们认为，除了坚固性——即维特鲁威所引入的三个基本品质中的另一个，建筑应该主要是功能性的，即实用性的东西。坚固性是指建筑是坚实的和持久的，而实用性是指建筑（例如庙宇）的功能及其为使用者提供的保护的一般用途。对于维特鲁威和一般的经典哲学来说，这个三元体被视为一个统一体：善和美似乎必然联系在一起，或者至少它们的和谐似乎是需要努力实现的理想。（因此，理想的人被视为具有道德和审美的品质，他是英俊和勇敢的——Kalos kai agathos，正如自希罗多德（Herodotus）以来的传统所说的那样）。这个和谐的理想仍然指导着阿尔伯蒂，他对美的定义在前文当中已经被引用过了，即："美是一个物体内部所有部分之间的理性的和谐，增之一分则多，减之一分则少，任何一点点改变都只会让它变得糟糕"[阿尔伯蒂，1998 年]。

但是在包豪斯（Bauhaus）学院富有影响力的教学中，至少在某些阶段，功能被赋予了主要角色。1928 至 1930 年间，导演汉斯·迈耶（Hannes Meyer，1889–1954）写道：

建筑是一个技术过程而不是审美过程，房子的艺术性构建已经一次又一次违背了其实用功能。我们的房子如果按理想的、基本的原则来规划，应该变成一台机器。[55]

Unlike Le Corbusier, therefore, who, as we have seen, while claiming that a house was a "machine for living in" was clear that architects were artists who manipulated the functional ingredients of mere building to create architecture, Meyer sees no place for art at all. In his 1928 essay, *Bauen*, he claimed "all art is composition and thus anti-functional".[56]

However, others have always been more doubtful about the unity of good, that is firm and useful, and beautiful architecture. Each area took on a more autonomous status – and thus reflection began about how to bring the two together. That the beautiful is distinguished from the good by "not being useful" was stated in the enlightenment by Karl Philipp Moritz [Moritz, 1788, p. 11]. He derived this idea from the Abbé Charles Batteux who introduced an influential distinction between the *fine* and the *useful* arts (giving architecture a special position between the two) [1746]. And Kant famously stressed the difference between the good and the useful when he demanded that aesthetic judgements should be without selfinterest, abstracted from utilitarian concerns [Kant, 1790]. This line of reflection led to the aesthetic ideal of a *l'art pour l'art*: artworks should not be tainted by any functionality. "All art is quite useless" said Oscar Wilde [Wilde, 1990, p. 17]. Applied to architecture, this would mean that only the decorative elements of a building would contribute to its aesthetic character. The shape and form of a building may be determined by their function, but ornaments give the freedom of artistic expression. In an architectural textbook from 1865 we read that architecture is "nothing more or less than the art of ornamented and ornamental construction" (cited in [Gauldie, 1969, p. 3]). Yet, as we have seen, whether there should be any ornament in addition to the structure became a much debated issue in the twentieth century, when the "truthfulness" of decoration was challenged. In a certain way, this functionalist ideal recaptures the classic *kalos kai agathos* by bringing beauty and goodness together again. However, the lead is taken by the good (which is identified with the functional in modernity) because simply *by being functional* things are seen as beautiful – this is not quite the classic type of unity.

There are two fundamental reasons why this attempt in the twentieth century to reconcile utility and beauty are unconvincing. On the one side, the functional demands will always be underdetermined. Any building has a multitude of functions so that any design decision involves choosing which function to privilege. Even the mechanistic definition of a house as "a machine for living in" implies the "housing" of many different activities. We require shelter, entrances and exists, sanitary installations and noise protection, but also fresh air, and the right space for the things we want to do in a dwelling. But beyond this, there are many more functions that we need to satisfy: the ethical questions referred to earlier such as being "green", or improving (or at least not impeding) people's psychological well-being by paying, for example, due regard to their life-style and traditions. Any architect will have to make many functional trade-offs – and the resulting buildings will look very different, even if they have the same function. Heidegger was surely right in bringing "living" and "thinking" together: any building design is connected with a certain attitude to how we are to live.

因此，不同于勒·柯布西耶（正如我们已经了解的那样，他虽然声称房子是一个"生活于其中的机器"，但也清楚地知道，建筑师是艺术家，他们对本身不过是功能性的建筑材料进行操作，而创造出了建筑），迈耶完全不给艺术留空间。在他 1928 年的文章《建筑》（Bauen）中，他声称"所有的艺术都是作品创作，因此是反功能的"。[56]

然而其他人一直更为怀疑善的统一性，即稳固的、有用的并且美的建筑。每个主题都具有更加自主的地位——因此人们开始反思如何将两个主题结合在一起。美是"无用"的，这是它与善的区别，这是卡尔·菲利普·莫里茨在启蒙运动中说的[莫里茨，1788 年，第 11 页]。 他的这种思想源自阿贝·查尔斯·巴托（Abbé Charles Batteux），后者在精美的艺术和有用的艺术之间做了一个很有影响力的区分（建筑被赋予了一个位于这两者之间的特殊位置）[1746 年]。众所周知，康德强调善与有用性之间的区别，他认为美学判断不应该涉及自身利益，而应该从功利主义的考量中抽离出来 [康德，1790 年]。这种反思带来了艺术的美学理想：艺术品不应被任何实用性所污染。"所有的艺术都是没用的，"奥斯卡·王尔德（Oscar Wilde）这样说 [王尔德，1990 年，第 17 页]。应用到建筑中，这就意味着一栋建筑物只有它的装饰性元素能够实现其美学特征。建筑物的形状和形式可能由它们的功能来决定，但是建筑物的装饰提供了艺术表达的自由。在一本 1865 年的建筑教科书中我们可以读到，建筑"完全就是被装饰的、又带来装饰效果的艺术"（引自 [高迪尔（Gauldie），1969 年，第 3 页]）。然而，正如我们已经知道的，在结构以外是否应该有任何装饰物，在二十世纪成为一个非常有争议的问题，当时装饰的"真实性"受到挑战。在某种程度上，这种功能主义的理想通过再次将美和善结合起来，重新找回了经典的"美与善合二为一"（kalos kai agathos）。但是，善（在现代善与功能性密切相关）应处于主导的地位，因为事物只要具备功能性，就可以认为是美的——这并不完全符合经典的统一性范式。

二十世纪这种调和实用性和美的尝试为何不足以令人信服，有两个根本原因。一方面，功能需求从来都不能被完全确定。任何建筑都有许多功能，因此任何设计决策都涉及到选择优先照顾哪个功能。即使是机械式地将房子定义为"在其中生活的机器"，这种定义也暗示了在"住所"内要开展许多不同的活动。我们需要庇身之处、进口和出口、卫生设施和噪音防护，也需要新鲜的空气，还需要适当的空间去开展我们想在住宅里做的那些事情。但是除此之外，我们还有许多其他功能需要满足：包括前面提到的道德问题，如绿化，或者通过适当地照顾人们的生活方式和传统来改善（或者至少不妨碍）他们的心理健康。任何建筑师都必须进行许多功能方面的权衡——由此产生的建筑物在外表上大不相同，即使它们具有相同的功能。在将"生活"和"思想"融合在一起这方面，海德格尔无疑是正确的：任何建筑设计都与我们将如何生活的特种态度联系在一起。

Secondly, even if function could be precisely determined, the form of buildings that meet that function is by no means determined, which is obvious when we consider the wide variety of styles that have been justified on the grounds of their being functional. These range from gothic cathedrals (according to Pugin and Ruskin) to the City for Three Million People that Le Corbusier advocated. Forms cannot be deduced in an algorithmic process. We have different materials (stone, concrete, metal, wood), we have different forms (round, square columns, walls) and even styles that could all fulfil the same function in a good way. What we regard as an adequate form to house a function is as much determined by our expectations and traditions. Arthur Schopenhauer (in empathetic vein) remarks that columns must be designed bigger than it is necessary for the static function because only then are we "absolutely reassured" that they will not break [Schopenhauer, 1859, Vol. 2, p. 390].

It might come as no surprise that the debate about form and function has become less vivid in recent years. It has proved impossible to reach an uncontroversial agreement on the connection between beauty and utility. Disagreement remains on all levels: what is the appropriate theory on which to base a view? Is it 'objectively' right to try to make the form follow a function? If so, which function? And what of beauty? Can there be a beauty merely arising out of meeting functional needs? And, how are we to make design decisions in face of a plurality of heterogenous demands and values (moral values, economical values, functional demands)? Architectural Aesthetics seems to inherit and unite the philosophical problems of many, if not all normative theories.

But if architecture mirrors many of the debates and tensions of philosophy, could it in itself provide some kind of mediation between apparently irreconcilable positions? In the past it has been thought of as an embodiment of philosophical insights. "Humanity has lost its dignity; but Art has rescued it and preserved it in significant stones", Friedrich Schiller famously wrote [Schiller, 1795, 9th letter]. Such mediation would be most evident in the scale and style of a building in an urban setting: a building or set of buildings might mediate between a set of aesthetic ideas and create a kind of synthesis. In the nineteenth century, a time, as we have seen, of stylistic eclecticism, certain architects, like Karl Friedrich Schinkel, thought very hard about the meanings that could be attached to particular styles.[57] His Neues Museum in Berlin, for example, combines a classic Greek façade with elements of the bourgeois architecture of nineteenth century Berlin, and thus speaks about the possibility of harmonizing a modern culture with classic ideals. In more recent practice, buildings which are clearly contemporary in expression and are placed in an historic context in such a way as to enhance it, and allow us to re-read it differently, may be appreciated similarly. Norman Foster's gallery at Nîmes, opposite the Roman Maison Carré, has been interpreted in this way, as has the Piano and Rogers design of the Centre Pompidou in Paris. In his influential *Collage City*, the critic Colin Rowe suggested that the quality of a great city like Rome could be explained precisely because it represented a "collision of utopias", rather than a fully executed single vision – implying that this mediating ability of architecture was one of its most important cultural contributions, and that architects might proceed by a process of *bricolage* [Rowe and Koetter, 1978].

其次，即使功能可以被精确地界定，但是满足该功能的建筑物形式却无法确定，考虑到各种不同的风格都已经合理地证明了其功能性，这一点非常明显。这些风格范围广泛，从哥特式大教堂（据普金和罗斯金（Pugin and Ruskin））到勒·柯布西耶所倡导的三百万人的城市。形式不能通过算法过程推导出来。我们有不同的材料（石头、混凝土、金属、木材），我们有不同的形式（圆形、方柱、墙），甚至不同的风格，都可以很好地实现同一个功能。我们所认为的满足某个功能的恰当形式同样取决于我们的期望和传统。亚瑟·叔本华（Arthur Schopenhauer）（以移情的方式）指出，柱子必须设计得比固位功能所需要的更大，因为只有那样，我们才能"绝对安心"，认为它们不会折断 [叔本华，1859 年，第 2 卷，第 390 页]。

　　关于形式和功能的辩论在过去几年中已变得不那么热烈了，这或许不足为奇。就美与实用性之间的关系达成毫无争议的一致观点，已经证明是不可能的了。分歧仍然存在于各个层面：形成一个观点所依据的适当理论是什么？努力让形式效力于某种功能，是否在"客观上"是正确的？如果是，应该是哪种功能呢？而美又如何呢？是否可能单单满足了功能需求便产生了某种美？而且，面对多种不同类型的需求和价值观（道德价值、经验价值、功能需求），我们如何进行设计决策？建筑美学似乎继承和融合了许多（如果不是所有的）规范理论的哲学问题。

　　但是，如果所建筑映射出许多的哲学辩论和争论，那么它本身是否能够在明显不可调和的立场之间提供某种调解呢？在过去，建筑被认为是哲学见解的一个实例。"人类已经失去了它的尊严，但是艺术挽救了它，并将它保存在重要的石材之中，"这是弗里德里希·席勒（Friedrich /Schiller）曾写过的一句名言 [席勒，1795 年，第九封信]。这样的调解作用在城市环境下的建筑物规模和风格中体现得最为明显：建筑物或建筑物集群可能调和了一系列的美学思想，创建出一个综合体。在十九世纪——正如我们所知道的，这是一个风格折中主义的时代，某些建筑师（像卡尔·弗里德里希·申克尔）苦思冥想附加到特定风格之上的意义。57 例如，他位于柏林的新博物馆（Neues Museum in Berlin）将经典的希腊式外墙与十九世纪柏林的资产阶级建筑元素结合起来，因此表明了协调现代文化与经典理想的可能性。我们还可以从类似的角度去欣赏近年来那些表现手法明显是现代风格、又被置于历史环境中以达到强化的效果、允许我们以不同的方式做出重新解读的建筑物。人们用这种方式去解读诺曼·福斯特位于尼姆市、在罗马卡雷神庙（Roman Maison Carré）对面的画廊，还有皮亚诺（Piano）和罗杰斯（Rogers）设计的巴黎蓬皮杜中心。在其富有影响力的作品《拼贴城市》（Collage City）中，评论家柯林·罗（Colin Rowe）建议，像罗马这样的伟大城市的品质得以被人们精确地阐释，因为它代表了一种"乌托邦式的冲突"，而不是一个被完全付诸实践的单一愿景——这暗示了建筑的这种调解能力是其最重要的文化贡献之一，并且建筑师可能通过一个零星修补的过程继续进行这种调解 [罗和克特尔（Koetter），1978 年]。

Naturally we can find such an ability to mediate or synthesize in many other areas of artistic activity. But architecture serves so many needs and functions at once that its answers appear to be more developed and richer than those of other arts. In particular, architecture must always provide a (practical) answer of how to integrate functional and other claims. As in other areas, whether the philosophical difficulties it throws up are seen as essentially problematic, or a possible contribution to reconciling profound difficulties in our culture and thinking, will depend on the position different people adopt.

Aesthetics and Ethics

While the tensions between formal and functional demands are much discussed in literature, not much ink has been spilled on the clash between formal and moral conflicts that architecture can face. Sometimes a morally better solution is aesthetically less pleasing – the insulation of the walls of historic buildings for the sake of a reduced energy consumption is an obvious example. To clarify this issue we ask more generally: what sort of conflicts are to be expected in the design-area between moral and aesthetic demands? And why are they so difficult to solve?

A well-known difficulty of any clash of normative demands is that there are quantitative issues, which are calculable with reasonable precision, and qualitative issues, which are not amenable to the same kind of measurement. How these demands should be balanced against each other is hard to decide, in particular if the very idea of "balancing" is biased towards quantifiable issues. This is a general problem, but has particular characteristics for architecture, which is susceptible to both types of demands. Certainly, architecture faces many demands with unquantifiable criteria. Think about a concept like "beauty". Whereas visual comfort, or the use of materials that are warm to the touch, may be matters that can be quantified, whether the aesthetic quality of a conjunction of particular sets of forms is quantifiable remains questionable.[58] In a similar way, we could say that it is easy to measure whether we have or have not met some ethical demands; but there are others that are less objectively measurable. We are therefore faced with a complex of categorically different criteria even within the same type of demands.

And these demands are not hierarchically ordered in an obvious way: For example, we cannot simply argue that only those buildings that perform satisfactorily in all *measurable* ways get themselves into the category where they can be judged in *incommeasurable* ways, because we can all think of buildings that fail in some measurable way, but are nevertheless highly regarded for good reasons (Le Corbusier's famous *Villa Savoye* would be an example: it seems impossible to waterproof it). That a building is successful technically, on the other hand, is no guarantee that it is going to be of a high architectural standard.

What makes things even more intriguing is that there are further demands of other types, and morality itself demands a respect for multiple demands in architecture. Budgetary prudence, for example, could be a reasonable criterion for a client commissioning

当然，我们可以在艺术活动的许多其他领域找到这样一种调解或融合的能力。但是建筑需要同时满足诸多需求和功能，以致于它提供的答案似乎比其他艺术提供的答案更为发达和丰富。尤其是建筑必须始终为如何整合功能性要求和其他要求提供一个（实际）答案。与其他领域一样，它所提出的哲学难题会被看作是从根本上就是有问题的，还是被看作可能对调解我们文化和思想的深刻难题有所贡献，这将取决于不同的人们所采取的立场。

美学和伦理学

虽然形式要求和功能要求之间的冲突已经在文献中有过许多讨论，但是关于建筑所面临的形式与道德之间的冲突的论著却并不多见。有时，道德意义上更好的解决方案在美学上却不那么令人愉快——为减少能源消耗起见的历史建筑物采用的隔热材料就是一个明显的例子。为了阐明这个问题，我们可以从更广义的层面发问：在设计领域，道德需求与审美需求之间预计会有什么样的冲突？它们为何这么难以解决？

关于规范性需求冲突中一个众所周知的难题，是其中既有以合理的精确度进行计算的定量问题，也有不适合采用同样衡量方法的定性问题。如何在这些需求之间达到相互平衡是很难抉择的，特别是当"平衡"这个想法本身就偏向于定量的问题时。这是一个普遍存在的问题，但是对于建筑而言具有特别的特征，建筑易受到以上两种需求类型的影响。当然，建筑面临的许多需求有着无法量化的标准。试想一下某个概念，例如"美"。虽然视觉舒适性或者使用触摸上去比较温暖的材料或许是可能量化的事物，但是是否可以量化特定形式的组合拼接所具有的美学品质，仍然存在着疑问。[58] 同样地，我们可以说，衡量我们是否已经或尚未满足某些道德要求是很容易的，但是还有其他事物客观上是不太好衡量的。因此，即使在同一类型的需求中，我们也面临着复杂的不同类别的标准。

这些需求并不能明显地分出等级次序：例如，我们不能简单地认为，只有那些在所有可衡量的方式上表现得令人满意的建筑才能归入到价值不可衡量的作品类别之中，因为我们全都可以列举出一些建筑物，它们在某种可衡量的方式上令人失望，但尽管如此，它们仍然以充分的理由获得了很高的评价（勒·柯布西耶著名的萨伏伊别墅就是一个例子：似乎不可能让它防水。）另一方面，建筑在技术上的成功并不能保证它具有较高的建筑水准。

使事情变得更加有趣的是，还有其他类型的更多的需求，而道德本身要求尊重建筑当中的多重需求。例如，预算审慎可以是客户委托

architects, and the constraints that lead to that demand could be quite precisely measured – if the client is a charity, say, with a limited budget. But we know that many of the acknowledged masterpieces were only achieved because architects were in some sense irresponsible with their client's money in the service of a greater ideal – namely creating a work of architecture that transcended its immediate context – which we would find hard to quantify. The issue of flexibility, however, which would seem to be reasonably easy to measure objectively, is interesting. From a user's point of view, the adaptability of buildings is certainly advantageous, so that making buildings that are capable of adaptation could be a criterion for architectural worth. There are many examples of buildings that have been converted satisfactorily from one use to another: the power station on London's South Bank, for example, into an art gallery, Tate Modern. There is an analogy here with a concept like "freedom": human autonomy is morally good, though it allows for immoral choices. Accepting the brief for making a former social housing complex (like the *Cité de la Muette*) into a concentration camp is ethically repulsive. But it is dangerous to blame the architect for the choice some future user makes, though it is clear that some forms of building design allow themselves to be reinterpreted more easily for questionable purposes.[59] But flexibility can also be complicated in aesthetic terms if we hold a classical theory that a great work of architecture is defined as that to which nothing can be added or taken away except for the worse [Alberti 1988].

The resulting picture is highly complex: We have tensions between different types of demands (moral, aesthetic, economic) and between quantifiable and unquantifiable. And because the different demands are deeply interwoven, we cannot even have a trade-off on the level of quantifiable demands, because we can have (more or less) quantifiable moral demands to obey unquantifiable normative demands of other types (e.g. to be economically responsible) – and unquantifiable moral demands to obey quantifiable demands of other types (e.g. for flexible buildings). Architecture has not come up with a timeless solution to the tensions between different demands; their clash seems therefore to be an ongoing theme of architectural self-reflection.

Taylor and Levine claim that the study of the intersection of architecture and ethics enables one to "achieve a more comprehensive understanding of architecture and ethics than traditionally conceived by either moral philosophers or architectural theorists (particularly phenomenologists) alone". The authors want to see aesthetic issues as an integral part of the function of a building: it would be impossible therefore to design a war memorial that was aesthetically successful if it could also be seen as endorsing an immoral politics. But as we have observed there are well-known instances of (what most people would consider to be) significant works of architecture that were designed to serve autocratic regimes, or contain uses that we would hardly sanction today: the *Alhambra*, or the *Coliseum*, or Terragni's *Casa del Fascio* at Como. According to the authors, the prospects for philosophical investigation are limited, in any case, since they "question the effectiveness of philosophical enquiry, as commonly practised, for understanding moral values in relation to the built environment" [Taylor and Levine 2011 p.78].

建筑师时的一个合理准则，引发该需求的各种限制因素也可以非常精确地进行衡量——比如说客户是一个预算有限的慈善机构。[59] 但是我们知道，许多公认的杰作能够问世，就是因为建筑师为实现一种更伟大的理想而在某种意义上对其客户的资金不负责任——即创造了一个超越其当下环境的的建筑作品，我们发现这是很难量化的。然而，灵活度的问题是很有趣的，这似乎可以很容易客观地进行衡量。从用户的角度来看，建筑物的适应改造性当然是有益的，因此筑造能够适应改造的建筑物可以是衡量建筑价值的一个标准。有许多建筑物的例子，它们已经以令人满意的方式从一种用途转换为另一种用途：例如，伦敦南岸的发电站被转换成一座画廊——泰特现代艺术馆。关于"自由"之类的概念，有一个比喻：人的自主性在道德上是善的，尽管它允许人做不道德的选择。接受一份把社会住房建筑群（如 Cité de la Muette）改造为集中营的工作，在道德上是令人厌恶的。但是，因为某个将来的用户所做的选择而去责怪建筑师，则是危险的，尽管很显然某些建筑设计形式自身更容易被重新解读，用做人们难以接受的用途。但是如果我们坚持古典理论，认为伟大的建筑增之一分则多、减之一分则少、任何改变只会让它变糟糕，那么美学上的灵活度也可以说是很复杂的 [阿尔伯蒂，1988 年]。

由此产生的局面非常复杂：在不同类型的要求（道德要求、审美要求、经验要求）之间，以及在可量化与不可量化的要求之间，都存在着争议。由于不同的要求是相互密切交织在一起的，我们甚至在可量化的要求这个层面上都无法达成一致，因为我们会有（或多或少）可量化的道德要求以便遵从其他类型的不可量化的规范性要求（例如在经济上负责），也会有不可量化的道德要求以便遵从其他类型的可量化的要求（例如，关于具有灵活度的建筑物）。建筑学尚未对不同要求之间的冲突提出一个一劳永逸的解决方案；因此这些需求之间的冲突看来将成为建筑学自我反思的一个持续的主题。

泰勒（Taylor）和莱文（Levine）声称，对建筑学与伦理学交叉领域的研究使得人们能够"取得比传统上单独由道德哲学家或建筑理论家（特别是现象学家）所取得的更加全面的、对建筑学与伦理学的理解"。这两位作者希望将美学问题作为建筑物功能的一个组成部分：因此，不可能设计出一个美学上成功的、同时在人们看来是在支持不道德政治的战争纪念馆。但是，正如我们所观察到的，有一些著名的、（大多数人认为是）重要的建筑作品的实例，这些作品旨在服务于专制政权，或者包含了我们今天难以认同的用途：阿罕布拉（Alhambra），或罗马斗兽场（Coliseum），或位于科莫的法西斯大厦（Terragni's Casa del Fascio）。在这两位作者看来，哲学探讨注定是前景有限的，因为关于"人们通常为了理解与建筑环境有关的道德价值而提出的哲学问题"，两位作者"对这一哲学问题的有效性提出了质疑"[泰勒和莱文，2011 年，第 78 页]。

Beauty as an ideal of architecture

In the previous sections, we have given an account of aesthetic debates, categories, and the problem of heterogeneous demands that architecture faces. It is noteworthy that "beauty", for millennia the central notion of Aesthetics, is merely one of several categories in contemporary debates and not even a highly respected one: The study of beauty, let alone the demand to design and erect beautiful buildings, has fallen from grace in contemporary Aesthetics. Most architects would clearly oppose any demand that they should design beautiful buildings. We find several objections against an orientation of art (and architecture) towards beauty.

A general doubt was raised by John A. Passmore in the 1950es, when he stressed that beauty seems metaphysically "suspect" because it seems to suggest an escape from reality (or at least what most consider reality to be): "'Beauty' is always nice; always soothing; [...] it is the refuge of the metaphysician finding a home for art in his harmonious universe [...]" [Passmore, 1954]. Theodor W. Adorno and others gave this objection a political turn by arguing that beauty is politically dangerous: It promotes an uncritical, affirmative approach to the existing social world. After the decline of religion, beauty seems the new "opium of the people" (to re-use Marx's famous phrase).

Does beauty really make people accept unjust, exploitative or generally bad situations too easily? To be sure, beauty (and beauties) *can* be seductive and promote escapes from reality – and it is often used for this purpose. Stalin's Palace of Culture and Science in Warsaw, the glamorous casinos of Las Vegas and the CCTV-tower in Bejing can certainly be interpreted as attempts to persuade people by aesthetic means into an uncritical pro-attitude to the *status quo* of the state, the economical situation or some institution. And psychological research backs this observation at least in principle: It can show that facial beauty, for example, has an "automatic influence on people's responses [...] and elicit(s) positive evaluative responses" [van Leeuwen and Macrae, 2004].

However, the Passmore-Adorno objection is still not convincing. First, it all depends on what exactly is affirmed by some beautiful artifact or building. Wright's Fallingwater, pleasingly blended into its natural setting, has been praised as the architect's "most beautiful job" by [*Time*, 1938]; and its beauty can encourage people to have an intensified relationship to the natural environment (Wright describes this as an ideal of "organic architecture" [Wright 1954, p.3]). There seems nothing objectionable if beauty 'seduces' people to do good things. Beauty, for example, has been used to make education and scholarship attractive (Christopher Wren's Trinity College library in Cambridge) or to strengthen people's support of democracy and lead them to political engagement (Louis Kahn's National Parliament of Bangladesh). Architecture is like real life: being seduced by the right beautiful woman (e. g. one's own wife) with a good intention (e.g. love) and for a good purpose (e.g. happiness) is not objectionable at all. Passmore's more general suspicion that beauty lulls people into a wrong metaphysical approach is rather problematic for similar reasons.

美作为建筑的一种理想

在前面的章节中，我们已经论述了关于美的争论、美的种类以及由于建筑面临多种不同类型的需求而带来的问题。值得注意的是，作为几千年来美学之中心概念的"美"，在当代讨论中仅仅是几种类别当中的一个，甚至都不是特别被尊重的一个概念；对美的研究——更不用说去要求设计和建造美的建筑——在当代美学中已经黯然失色。大多数建筑师明确反对他们应该设计美丽的建筑之类的任何要求。我们发现有几种针对以美为导向的艺术（和建筑）的反对意见。

二十世纪五十年代，约翰·帕斯莫尔（John A. Passmore）强调从形而上学角度来看美是可疑的，因为它似乎暗示一种对现实（或者至少是大多数人认为是现实中的某种事物）的逃避，当时他提出了一个具有普遍意义的疑问："'美'始终是好的；始终是抚慰人心的；……它是形而上学者们的避难所，他们要在自己的和谐宇宙中为艺术寻得一个家园……"[帕斯莫尔，1954 年]。狄奥多·阿多诺（Theodor W. Adorno）和其他人把这种反对意见引向了政治层面，认为美在政治上是危险的：它促使人们对现有社会世界持一种不加批判的、肯定的态度。宗教衰落以后，美似乎成了新的"人民鸦片"（这里再次使用了马克思的名言）。

美是否真的使人们太易于接受不公正的、剥削性的或大多不好的情况？可以肯定的是，美（美的事物）可以是诱人的，并促使人们逃避现实——美也经常被用于这一目的。斯大林的华沙文化科学宫、拉斯维加斯迷人的赌场和北京的中央电视台塔楼，确实可以被解释为试图利用美学手段说服人们对国家的现状、经济形势或某些机构持一种不加批判的赞成态度。而心理学研究至少在原则上支持上述观点：它可以证明，（例如）面部美"自动影响着人们的反应……并引发积极的评价反馈"[范·鲁凡（Van Leeuwen）和麦克雷（Macrate），2004 年]。然而，帕斯莫尔—阿多诺提出的对美的反对意见仍然不能令人信服。首先，这完全取决于美的作品或建筑到底在倡导什么。赖特（Wright）的"流水别墅"——很好地融入了它的自然环境中——被[时代周刊，1938 年]誉为建筑师"最美丽的工作"；并且它的美可以鼓励人们加强与自然环境的关系（赖特将这描述为一种"有机建筑"的理想）[赖特，1954 年，第 3 页]。如果美能"诱使"人们去做好的事情，那么似乎就没有什么值得反对的。例如，美已经被用来使教育和奖学金变得有吸引力（克里斯托弗·雷恩（Christopher Wren）的剑桥大学三一学院图书馆）或加强人们对民主的支持并使他们参与民主政治活动（路易斯·康（Louis Kahn）的孟加拉国国民议会）。建筑就像现实生活一样：怀着好的动机（例如爱）、为寻求正确的目的（例如幸福）而被合适的美丽女人（例如自己的妻子）所诱惑，完全不令人反感。帕斯莫尔在更广泛的层面上怀疑美诱使人们采取错误的形而上学的态度，这种怀疑也是很有问题的，理由与上文类似。

Neither is it obvious whether the fashionable worldview of today is the last word of metaphysics (after all, there are many different worldviews presented by philosophy and religions). Nor is it uncontroversial whether art must mirror the world as it is. It could also aim at presenting a better reality (a harmonious one, for example) in an attractive way so that people are motivated to improve states of affairs. Beauty can move us in all sorts of directions, so why not in good ones? Secondly, the objection is based upon an over-simplified motivational theory.

We can agree that beauty sometimes makes people accept something too easily – but it can also produce an increased level of awareness or receptivity to the world, and a strong sensitivity for its problems. Friedrich Schiller famously argued that art and the aesthetic impulse (including beauty) allow the individual to transcend inner and outer constraints, and thus increase his or her freedom rather than being a means of suppression.

A second objection against beauty in art and architecture is directed against its allegedly simplistic nature. Beauty cannot grasp complex aesthetic phenomena like the ugly, as Nelson Goodman amongst others, have argued. He writes in his *Languages of Art*:

> Folklore has it that a good picture is pretty. At the next higher level, pretty is re-placed by 'beautiful', since the best pictures are often obviously not pretty. But again, many of them are in the most obvious sense ugly. If the beautiful excludes the ugly, beauty is no measure of aesthetic merit; but if the beautiful may be ugly, then 'beauty' becomes only an alternative and misleading word for aesthetic merit" [Goodman, 1976, p. 255].

Goodman's point, however, is mainly about the use of language, it seems. If the term "beauty" is reserved for simplistically pleasing, lovely features, then he is obviously right. Then "beauty" should be contrasted with "aesthetic merit" as soon as the artwork's attraction is more complex and includes tensions or disturbing elements. But it seems more appropriate to talk about "kitsch" where Goodman talks about "beauty". Great artworks are never so simplistic and their beauty is certainly more demanding. They offer a rich sensual experience with very different elements, even painful, ugly or dis-turbing, but in a manner so that everything is in its place and the overall effect is there-fore pleasing – thus beautiful. The (beautiful) Greek tragedies, for example, do contain sad and disturbing scenes like murder, and Auguste Rodin's (beautiful) *Gates of Hell* shows many distorted beings.

As Ruth Lorand writes about Matisse's *Blue Nude* (1907): "Indeed, the woman por-trayed in the painting is not very pretty, the lines are not delicate, and most classical conventions are violated. But the painting is beautiful! Its beauty lies in its order that integrates sensual as well as conceptual elements, and offers thereby a new interpre-tation of these elements. Whatever makes it a good or great work also makes it beau-tiful." [Loran, 2007]

当今流行的世界观是否就是形而上学的最终版本，这尚不明确（毕竟哲学和宗教提出了许多不同的世界观），而且关于艺术是否必须反映真实的世界，这一点上也不是没有争议。艺术也可以致力于以一种富有吸引力的方式呈现一个更好的现实（例如一个和谐的现实），从而推动人们改善现状。美可以推动我们涌向各个方向，那么为什么不选择正确的方向呢？其次，对美的反对意见基于一种过度简单化的动机理论。我们同意美有时使人们太容易接受某些事物，但是它也可以使人们提高对世界的认识或接纳程度，并使得人们对世界所存在的问题十分敏感。弗里德里希·席勒有一句名言，认为艺术和审美冲动（包括美）使得个人超越内部和外部约束，从而增加了他或她的自由，而不是成为一种压制手段。

针对艺术和建筑美的第二种反对意见着眼于所谓的美的简单化性质。纳尔逊·古德曼（Nelson Goodman）等人认为，美不能抓住复杂的美学现象，如丑陋。他在《艺术语言》（Languages of Art）中这样写道：

"按民间说法，一幅好图片很漂亮。在下一个更高的层次上，漂亮被'美丽'所取代，因为最好的图片通常显然是不漂亮的。但是，这些图片中有许多是丑陋的，这是特别显而易见的。如果美丽不涵盖丑陋，那么美就不能衡量美学价值；但是如果美丽可以是丑陋的，那么'美'就只是关于美学价值的一个替代性且具有误导性的词语。"[古德曼，1976 年，第 255 页]

然而，古德曼的观点似乎主要是关于语言的使用的。如果"美"这个词专用于描绘那些单纯令人愉悦的、可爱的特征，那么他显然是对的。那么一旦艺术作品具有更加复杂的吸引力，且包含了冲突和令人不安的元素，"美"就与"美学价值"对立起来了。但是古德曼在谈论"美"的时候，说他谈论的是"媚俗"似乎更为合适。伟大的艺术作品从来不会如此简单，它们的美必定要求更高。它们以非常不同的元素，甚至痛苦、丑陋或令人不安的元素，提供丰富的感官体验，采用的方式是使每个事物各就其位，且整体效果是令人愉悦的——因此是美的。例如，（美丽的）希腊悲剧确实包含悲伤和令人不安的场景，如谋杀，奥古斯都·罗丹（Auguste Rodin）的（美丽的）地狱之门呈现了许多扭曲的生物。正如鲁斯·洛兰（Ruth Lorand）关于马蒂斯（Matisse）的《蓝色裸体》（Blue Nude）（1907 年）所写的那样："的确，画中所描绘的女人不是很漂亮，线条不够细腻，并且违反了大多数古典。但是这幅画是美丽的！它的美在于它的次序，融合了感官元素和概念元素，从而对这些元素做出了新的解读。任何使它成为一个好的和伟大的作品的东西，也使它变得美丽。"[罗兰（Loran），2007 年]

Does it also make sense to talk about architectural beauty in a more complex and demanding sense? To answer this question we should analyse in some more detail what architectural beauty amounts to. We suggest distinguishing five types, namely formal, functional, contextual, time-related, and intellectual. Let us look at them in turn.

1. Formal

The most commonly admired type of beauty is formal. This is the beauty that moves us when architects manipulate volumes to create memorable spaces – such as the Pantheon in Rome, which is based on a sphere, and which few visitors are unaffected by. For Pevsner, who has already been mentioned, and for many critics of his generation, architecture is primarily an art of space. Architects also assemble masses together, much as a sculptor sets out objects in light: this plastic manipulation of form was praised by Le Corbusier as the highest achievement of architecture. The careful articulation of the surfaces of buildings – their roughness and smoothness, and their detail – is also intrinsic to works of architecture.

2. Functional

Formal, or compositional, beauty can be found in other works of art, such as sculptures and pictures, but functional beauty is a quality found in the design of useful products, such as implements, and architecture. A well-made implement, or mechanism, has a beauty that is inherent in its efficient workings – we can think of the products of craft or engineering design [cf. Pye 2002]. In architectural environments the way that functional criteria are solved in elegant ways (such as the beautiful drainage system in St Marks' Square in Venice) gives a particular satisfaction that would not be achieved were the objects we are contemplating merely useless or decorative.

3. Contextual

Formal and functional beauty can be found in many artifacts – well-designed implements, or well-crafted products – not just in architecture. But architecture is almost always related to a particular location: it is situated in a context. Caravans, mobile homes, and pre-fabricated buildings may be less context-related (though even they should take account in their sitting of orientation to view and sunlight, and the climatic effect of the latitude in which they are to be placed), but most architecture enjoys what the Spanish architect Rafael Moneo has described as a "static immobility". And one of the principal tasks of the architect is therefore to learn to "listen to the murmur of the site" [Moneo 2004]. Or, to put it another way, architecture is an art of the "ensemble" [Neumeyer 1989]. The ways that effective architecture relates to its setting, whether urban or rural, and whether by seeking to blend in with it or stand out from it, is one of its most obvious characteristics, and most often a cause of criticism when people feel the wrong decision has been taken. In urban locations, the relationship to the immediate architectural context may be most important, and in any location architecture might well refer to its own antecedents – its cultural context.

在更复杂和更苛刻的意义上谈论建筑之美是否有意义？要回答这个问题，我们应更详细地分析建筑美实际上到底是什么？我们建议区分一个五种类型，即形式美、功能美、情境美、与时间相关的美和智力美。我们依次来看这些类型。

1. 形式美

最常见的美的类型是形式美。这是当建筑师操控体积以创造令人难忘的空间时感动我们的那种美，如罗马万神殿，它立足于一个圆形体，很少有访客不被其打动。对于佩夫斯纳（前面已经提到过他）和他那一代的许多批评家来说，建筑主要是一种空间艺术。建筑师还将各种物质聚集在一起，与雕塑家在光线中陈列物体非常类似：对形式的这种塑造操作被勒·柯布西耶称为建筑的最高成就。建筑物外表的精细呈现——它们的粗糙和平滑、以及它们的细节——也是建筑作品的内在元素。

2. 功能美

形式美或组合美可见于其他艺术作品，如雕塑和图片，但是功能美则是见于有用的产品（如工具和建筑）设计具有的一种品质。一个精心制作的工具或一个高效运作的机制有一种内在的美——我们可以试想一下工艺或工程设计的产品[参见派伊（Pye），2002 年]。在建筑环境中，功能标准通过优雅的方式得以解决（如威尼斯圣马克广场优美的排水系统），这给人一种特别的满足感；如果我们所构思的产品只是无用的或装饰性的，那么就不可能得到这种满足感。

3. 情境美

形式美和功能美可见于许多人工作品——精心设计的工具，或精心雕琢的产品，而不仅仅限于建筑。但是建筑几乎总是与特定的位置相关：它置身于某种环境之中。大篷车、移动房屋和预制组装型建筑可能与环境的关联较少（虽然它们也应该考虑安放时所朝向的视野和日光，以及其所处的纬度的气候影响），但是大多数建筑都具有西班牙建筑师拉菲尔·莫尼奥（Rafael Moneo）所描述的"静态不动性"，因此建筑师的主要任务之一是学习"倾听场地的低语"[莫尼奥，2004 年]。或者换句话说，建筑是"全体"的艺术[纽迈耶（Neumeyer，1989 年）]。实际的建筑与周围环境发生关联的方式——无论在城市或农村，无论是寻求与环境融合还是从中脱颖而出——是建筑最明显的特征之一，并且也是最常招致批评的一个原因，因为人们觉得这方面作出的决定是错误的。在城市地区，与直接的建筑环境的关系可能极其重要，而且在任何地方，建筑都可能会涉及其前身——即它的文化环境。

4. Time related

Since architecture tends to endure over many decades, or centuries, the way in which it succeeds in doing so is often a prime cause of the satisfaction it gives. The mere age of a building can give birth to aesthetic pleasures that might touch the sublime. And materials may be composed together so that they weather in a pleasing way, and the building grows old gracefully [Mostafavi, 1993]. At certain periods, the 'pleasing decay' of buildings has excited especial admiration: in the eighteenth century landscape garden, architects constructed ruins for the contemplation of their patrons. It is clear that the ageing of buildings over time may summon up pleasing associations. Materials that do not weather, on the other hand, need cleaning and re-finishing so as to preserve the newness that may be a necessary quality of some buildings. Just how much to repair, or restore, in ancient buildings, and how this should best be done, becomes a major issue for architects concerned with conservation.

5. Intellectual

There is a further type of beauty to a great work of architecture, similar perhaps to an elegant equation in mathematics, or the working through of a complex fugue in music, which we could call "intellectual". At a mundane level, highly-serviced buildings, which contain a systematic arrangement of ducts, and pipes meshed in such a way as not to inhibit the structure, would be an example of the satisfaction that can be obtained from working through a complex set of technical problems to an elegant solution. But more often we may find ourselves admiring buildings that employ a system of proportions which give a mathematical satisfaction, for example the war memorials and the unbuilt project for Liverpool Cathedral by Sir Edwin Lutyens (Radford 2008). Since buildings are complicated artifacts, the satisfactory resolution of a great variety of problems in a work of architecture is an intellectual achievement that is distinguishable from the formal beauty of the building itself, or its efficient performance. This is perhaps the most abstract, and complex, form of beauty.

These five types of architectural beauty allow us to understand why architectural beauty can (and should) aspire to be more than just pleasing. Successful architecture can be rather demanding, especially when we look at functional, time-related or intellectual beauty: To satisfy hygienic demands or to provide a drainage system does not automatically give rise to pleasing forms—yet a beautiful solution can be a pleasing way to deal even with unpleasant demands. The time-related beauty of building can include the cracks and damage, fading paintwork and distorted beams. Like an aged face, the facade of a house can have its own story to tell, has traces and irregularities that make it attractive and beautiful. And obviously, the intellectual beauty of a building will often be based upon the ways in which it answers difficult and unpleasant tasks. The National September 11 Memorial and Museum on Ground Zero, for example, does have grace and beauty not only due to its form, but also by giving an intellectually serious response to a horrible event: The two square pools at the place of the former Twin Towers is a remarkable reference to what has been lost.

4. 与时间相关的美

由于建筑可以历经几十年或几个世纪，它能成功地做到这一点，往往就是它带给人愉悦感的一个主要原因。仅仅是建筑物的年龄就可以让人们产生有望接近崇高的美学愉悦。材料可以组合在一起，以令人愉悦的方式经受风雨，建筑物优雅地老去[穆斯塔法维（Mostafavi），1993 年]。在某些时期，建筑物"令人愉悦的衰败"引起了人们特别的赞赏：在十八世纪的景观花园里，建筑师根据客户的意图修建了废墟。很明显，建筑物随着时间的推移的老化过程可能会唤起人们愉悦的联想。另一方面，不耐风雨的材料需要清洁和重新整理，以便保持崭新状态，这一状态可能是某些建筑物必须具备的品质。对于古代的建筑物，需要在多大程度上修复或重建，以及最好以何种方式修复或重建，成为关注建筑保护的建筑师们的一个重大课题。

5. 智力美

对于伟大的建筑作品来说，还有一种类型的美，它可能类似于数学里一个优雅的方程式，或者音乐中一首复杂的赋格曲编排，我们称之为"智力美"。在世俗的层面上，那些运转良好的建筑物对输送管道进行了系统性的布置，管线以不妨碍结构的方式彼此接合起来，可以说是通过解决一系列复杂的技术问题获得优雅的解决方案、从而给人带来愉悦感的一个实例。不过更多的时候，我们可能发现自己会欣赏那些采用了比例系统的建筑物，它们带给人数学上的愉悦感，例如战争纪念馆和由埃德温·卢森斯爵士（Sir Edwin Lutyens）设计的利物浦大教堂未完成的项目（拉德福（Radford），2008 年）。由于建筑物是复杂的人工作品，所以以令人满意的方式解决建筑作品中各种各样的问题，是一项智力成就，它有别于建筑本身的形式美或性能表现。这可能是最抽象的、复杂的美的形式。

这五种类型的建筑美使我们了解了建筑美为什么能够（并且应该）不仅仅是令人愉悦的。成功的建筑可以说是要求很高的，特别是当我们考虑到功能美、与时间相关的美或智力美时：满足卫生要求或者提供排水系统不会自动产生令人愉悦的形式——但是一个优美的解决方案可以以令人愉快的方式解决甚至不那么令人愉快的需求。建筑与时间相关的美可能包括裂缝和损坏、褪色的油漆和扭曲的横梁。与老人的脸一样，房子的外表能够诉说它自己的故事，那些痕迹和不合常规之处使它变得有吸引力而且优美。显然，建筑的智力美往往来自于它解决艰难的、令人不悦的任务的方式。例如，世贸大厦遗址上的国家 9·11 纪念碑和博物馆是优雅和美丽的，不仅因为它的形式，而且因为它对一个恐怖事件从理智上予以严肃的回应：位于前双子塔所在位置的两个方形水池，以不同寻常的方式诉说着所失去的一切。

Beauty, though often dismissed in architectural and aesthetic discourse, certainly deserves to be taken seriously again. After all, human beings long for it, and it is the challenge of art and architecture to satisfy this longing in a more demanding manner than kitsch will do. And, as is frequently pointed out, buildings are exposed to everyone. Whereas we do not have to pick up a prize-winning novel, or listen to a highly-praised piece of music, it is impossible to avoid the buildings all around us, and sometimes the ones that win awards may be the most difficult to appreciate. There is therefore an onus on architects to communicate in a way that, while it may be appreciated on many levels, is accessible, rather than conceived in a private language that only the *cognoscenti* can appreciate. This would involve a reconciliation, and a prioritisation of the types of beauty outlined above. Architects notoriously form a sub-culture, tending to find certain forms and materials (like bare concrete) beautiful, which the general public may find ugly and unfriendly. Yet, some would say it is part of architects' aesthetic duty to challenge the aesthetic expectations of clients – if they did not do so we would be condemned to a banal repetition of conventional buildings. The best architecture might well re-define what we call beautiful. Whilst it is arrogant for architects to say that people *must* learn to understand their buildings, it is clear that public taste develops and moves on, so that inspiring works of architecture broaden the area of acceptability for the general public. It is a principal task for architects, therefore, to judge carefully the accessibility of the buildings they propose, and this becomes one of the judgments between the five different types of beauty we identified above. It would seem that it is quite possible to have a formal beauty that is not functional, or particularly rigorous intellectually: this would be evident in a sculpturally compelling structure that was maybe not very useful, such as Zaha Hadid's fire station for the Vitra organisation. Buildings can also be formally beautiful, and work well, without being particularly satisfying in the fifth way: these might be "romantic" works, such as *Neuschwanstein*, the castle built by Ludwig II, that depend to a certain extent on the associations that are summoned up. But a building such as *Neuschwanstein* can be criticised if it is not also skilfully composed – it becomes merely kitsch. And a laboratory building that was rigorously worked through as a design, and also functioned well, would not necessarily be beautiful formally, even though at various periods architects have argued that we *ought* to find such buildings beautiful. Ideally, therefore, a beautiful building would represent some kind of unity of these five types of beauty. And this reconciliztion is what architects should aim at.

美，尽管经常在建筑和美学论述中被驳斥，但它确实值得被人们重新认真对待。毕竟，人类渴望它，艺术和建筑所面临的挑战是，用比媚俗作品更为苛刻的方式去满足人们的这种渴望。此外，正如人们经常指出的那样，建筑物暴露在每个人面前。虽然我们没必要拿起一本获奖的小说，或聆听一首被高度赞扬的乐曲，但是我们却无法回避周围所有的建筑物，而且，有时候那些获奖的建筑可能是最难欣赏的。因此，建筑师有责任以某种方式与人们交流，这种方式虽然可以从许多层面上去领会，但它是可以被人们理解的，而不是以只有行家才能理解的私密语言构思出来的。这将涉及对上述几种美的类型进行调和并优先排序。众所周知，建筑师们形成了一种亚文化，倾向于认为某些形式和材料（如清水混凝土）是美的，而一般公众可能会认为这些东西是丑陋的和不适宜的。然而，有人会说，挑战客户的审美预期是建筑师美学责任的一部分。如果建筑师不这样做，我们所面对的将全部是平凡重复的常规建筑。最好的建筑可能会以很好的方式重新定义我们所说的美的事物。虽然说若是建筑师们认为人们必须学会理解其建筑，这就显得有些自大了，但是很明显，公众的品味在不断发展和前进，所以富有启发性的建筑作品可以拓宽普通公众的接受能力范围。因此，建筑师的主要任务之一是仔细判断他们所提议的建筑物的易懂性，这成为关于我们上文所述的五种不同类型的美的评判标准之一。看来要获得一种非功能性的或是智力方面极其严谨的形式美，是非常有可能的：这一点在一个或许不是很有用、但雕刻引人注目的架构中是显而易见的，例如扎哈·哈迪德（Zaha Hadid）为维特拉（Vitra）组织设计的消防站。建筑物也可以是形式优美的、运作良好的，但并未在第五个方面让人觉得特别满意：这些建筑可能是"浪漫"的作品（如新天鹅城堡（Neuschwanstein）、路德维希二世（Ludwig II）建造的城堡），这些作品在某种程度上依赖于它们所引发的联想。但是像新天鹅城堡这样的建筑物，倘若同时也缺乏巧妙的构造，则会招致批评——它变得仅仅在媚俗罢了。而一个设计严谨同时运作良好的实验室建筑，在形式上不一定是优美的，哪怕是不同时期的建筑师们曾经认为我们理应发现这些建筑物是美的。因此，在理想状态下，一个优美的建筑将呈现出对以上五种类型的美的某种统一。这种调和统一是建筑师应追求的目标。

Philosophical positions illustrated in architectural practice

Three architects have been chosen to illustrate a variety of philosophical positions. Two practised in the twentieth century; the third continues to practice. Recent work has been selected for discussion, not because designs from earlier centuries do not illustrate a theory with equal clarity, but because the work of more contemporary designers is more likely to be relevant to the developing practice in the twenty-first century. It would be difficult to find practitioners whose work could be assigned exclusively to a particular position – even the most idealistic architects have to accommodate themselves to the circumstances of patronage in order to succeed in building anything. The position of many of them is difficult to unravel. The case of Le Corbusier has been mentioned already: his statements seem to exhibit a mechanistic positivism, but at the same time he stresses the primacy of art, and regarded himself as something of a Nietzschean *Übermensch*. We must also recall that these architects are not philosophers, although they may have read quite widely. The positions that they may claim that their buildings reflect could prove to be quite mistaken. But architects' misinterpretations of history have sometimes proved fruitful. Palladio's reconstructions of Roman houses would be an example: he believed, quite wrongly, that the houses of the rich were dignified by pediments. His own architecture, and the books he published illustrating it, had widespread influence and laid the foundations for "classical" domestic architecture throughout the western world. In a similar way, how architects interpret and make use of philosophical ideas in their practice, while it may not be technically correct, can have surprising repercussions.

Louis Kahn

The American architect Louis Kahn (1901-1974) represents one of the clearest examples of the position of the architect as platonic idealist. Although, as we swiftly discover with all the most interesting people, his background was complex and his cultural influences enormously wide, his idealist position is clear in what he built, in the procedures he adopted during design, in how he described his design process to students, and in what he wrote more generally about architecture [Benedikt, 1992; McCarter, 2005].

The sequence of five designs undertaken by Kahn's office between 1959 and 1967 for the Unitarian Church in Rochester, New Jersey, serves as an example of his design process. Kahn distinguished between what he called "form" and "design": "Form doesn't have shape or dimension. It simply has a kind of existence will",[60] he explained:

建筑实践中表明的哲学立场

我们选择了三位建筑师来说明多种不同的哲学立场。其中两位建筑师活跃于二十世纪；第三位迄今仍在执业。我们之所以选择这些较为近期的作品进行探讨，并非因为较早期的建筑设计不能同样清晰地阐述某种理论，而是因为更为现代的设计师的作品更有可能与二十一世纪正在发展中的实践相关。要找到能够将其作品归入某一特定立场的建筑师是很困难的，因为即便是最为理想主义的建筑师也不得不让自己作出改变，以适应资金情况从而顺利开展建造过程。很多建筑师的立场是不容易阐述清楚的。我们之前已提及勒·柯布西耶的案例：他的言论似乎展现出一种机械实证主义，但同时他也强调艺术的首要位置，并将自己视为类似于尼采所说的超人。我们还必须认识到这些建筑师并不是哲学家，尽管他们可能很博学。他们宣称的其建筑作品所反映的立场，可能最终被证明是完全错误的。但建筑师对于历史的错误解读有时反而有很好的效果。帕拉迪奥对罗马住宅的重建可以作为一个范例：他极其错误地认为，富人的住宅是通过山墙来体现其尊贵地位的。他自己的建筑作品以及他出版的相关书籍有着广泛的影响，并且奠定了西方世界"古典"民居建筑的基础。同样地，建筑师如何解读哲学理念，并在其实践中运用哲学理念，尽管从技术层面来讲也许并不正确，但也能带来出人意料的影响。

路易斯·康

美国建筑师路易斯·康（1901-1974）是柏拉图理想主义建筑师立场的一个典型范例。正如我们敏锐地在所有最有趣的人们身上发现的那样，路易斯·康的背景很复杂，他的文化影响力非常广泛。但是在他的建筑作品、他采取的设计流程、他向学生描述设计过程时所采用的方式以及他对于建筑的总体阐述中，都体现了非常明显的理想主义立场 [贝内迪克特，1992；麦卡特，2005]。

康的事务所于1959年至1967年之间关于新泽西州罗切斯特一神教堂所做的先后五次的设计，可以作为其设计流程的例证。康对他所说的"形式"和"设计"做了如下区分："形式是没有形状或维度的。它只是有一种存在的意志"，[60] 他解释道：

Form is impersonal. Design belongs to the designer. Design is a circumstantial act, how much money there is available, the site, the client, the extent of knowledge. Form has nothing to do with circumstantial conditions. In architecture, it characterises a harmony of spaces good for a certain activity of man. [Kahn, 1991, p. 113]

Kahn spoke frequently of "the institutions of man". It was the primary task of the architect to represent those institutions, whether museum, library, gallery, or school. His starting point, almost invariably, was with a simplified diagram which placed the primary element centrally and clustered subsidiary spaces around it. Kahn thus made a distinction between "served" and "servant" spaces. Geometry was used to reinforce the difference: the central space would be a clearly perceptible figure – a square or a circle, while the subsidiary spaces would adopt a more "circumstantial" geometry. Kahn therefore subscribes to Alberti's suggestion that a hierarchy of forms can help to symbolise the importance of different spaces. Kahn's earliest charcoal sketches assume such simplified geometries, but are far from precise in themselves – he is trying to get to the essence of the idea, and often it takes the work of many months, and the patient labour of his architectural assistants to discover, as it were, the final pattern in which the idea will realise itself. The drawings are in fact a process of meditation:

One may say that architecture is the thoughtful making of spaces. It is not the filling of areas prescribed by the client. It is the creating of spaces that evoke a feeling of appropriate use. [Kahn, 1991, p. 116]

In the case of Rochester Unitarian Church, the idea remains consistent through numerous iterations: the body of the church will be central, and around it cluster the several rooms that serve it – vestries, offices, porches and lobbies, cloakrooms, and boiler house, as well as the classrooms, for Kahn saw these as "serving" the central sanctuary. His clients, however, appeared to have favoured an arrangement similar to Frank Lloyd Wright's Unity Temple in Chicago, of 1906, which both in its brief and in its geometry presented a compelling precedent for the scheme. It is Kahn's persistence in holding on to his original concept, the "form", which gives the project much of its power. Some versions have a more dramatic expression of the central structure, especially the first with its truncated dome, reflecting Kahn's interest in the work of the engineer Buckminster Fuller. The body of the church is sometimes square, sometimes rectangular. Each version has an arcade around the church as an intermediate space, of greater or lesser elaboration; the first version, which is the most "ideal" geometrically, has an ambulatory as well as an arcade. Over an extended period of design and redesign, eventually a final version emerges, which reconciles the prescriptions of the client, and budgetary constraints, with the nature of the institution that it is the task of the architect to define: "The final design does not correspond to the first design though the form held" [Kahn, 1991, p. 116].

The process of design in which Kahn engaged acted as a powerful critique of the somewhat positivistic myth of functionalism evident in the proclamations of CIAM and

　　　　形式是不受个人影响的。设计则是属于设计者个人的。设计是一种与环境
　　相关的行为，可用的资金有多少，选址在哪里，客户是谁，知识范围怎样。而
　　形式与环境条件无关。在建筑中，形式以空间的和谐为特征，有利于人们在其
　　中开展特定活动。[康，1991，第113页]

　　康经常提到"人的机构"。他认为，建筑师的首要任务是代表这些机构，不
论是博物馆、图书馆、画廊，还是学校。他的设计基本上都是从一个简单的示意
图开始，示意图把主要元素放在中心位置，并让次要空间围绕在主要元素周围。
由此，康对"被服务"空间和"服务"空间进行了区分。他用几何学来强化这种
差异：中心空间是一个明显看得出来的图形，比如一个正方形或者圆形，而从属
空间则采用一种 "与环境更为相关" 的几何图形。因此康同意阿尔伯蒂的建议，
即可以用不同形式之间的层次去体现不同空间的重要性。康最早的炭笔素描设
计图呈现出这种简化的几何形状，但精确度还差得很远——早期他只是试图抓取
理念的精髓，而要确定实现理念的最终样式，通常需要数月的努力以及他的建筑
助理们耐心的劳动。这些图样实际上体现的是一种苦思冥想的过程：

　　　　人们可能会说，建筑是对空间进行深思熟虑的构建的过程。建筑并不是按
　　照客户的规定去把空间填满。建筑是对空间的创造，这些空间给人一种合理使
　　用的感觉。[康，1991，第116页]

　　在罗切斯特一神教堂的范例中，有一个理念在多次重复的工作得以贯穿始终：
教堂的主体位于正中，而服务于主体的一些房间围绕在主体周围，包括法衣室、
办公室、走廊和门厅、衣帽间、锅炉房以及教室，康将这些房间看做是"服务于"中
心主体的。但是他的客户似乎更青睐类似于弗兰克•劳埃德•赖特1906年设计的芝加
哥统一教堂的那种布局，该作品在建筑要求的阐述以及几何图形方面都开创了引
人瞩目的先例。康却坚持采用他最初的概念，即"形式"，为这个项目赋予了很
多力量。其中一些设计版本对中心结构的呈现更为戏剧化，特别是在第一个版本
中有一个被截短的圆形屋顶，反映了康对于工程师巴克敏斯特•富勒(Buckminster
Fuller)作品的兴趣。教堂的主体在一些版本里是正方形，在另一些版本里是矩形。
每个版本都有一个环绕教堂的拱廊作为中间区，只是在精细程度上有高低之分；
在几何学上最为"完美" 的第一个版本除了拱廊之外还有回廊。经过了一个较长
的设计和重新设计阶段，最终版本终于浮出水面，该版本兼顾了客户的要求、预
算的制约以及机构的性质，建筑师的任务是阐明："尽管形式保持不变，但最终
设计与初始设计并不相符"[康，1991，第116页]。
　　康的这一设计过程有力地批判了关于功能主义的所谓实证主义迷思，这种迷
思可见于国际现代建筑协会（CIAM）的声明，并

propounded by Walter Gropius and his followers. For them, building forms should arise spontaneously as a result of solving functional problems by means of modern technology; the resulting plan tended to be asymmetrical, and the structure lightweight.[61] Kahn's emphasis on the continuity of a conceptual idea harks back to the procedures of nineteenth century *Beaux Arts* architects, who, in the celebrated competitions for the Prix de Rome, first came up with an *esquisse*, a small sketch, which represented the primary design intentions, next proceeded to a *poché*, a pocket-sized set of drawings within which the design principles were embedded, and only in the third stage developed the detailed and beautiful drawings of the final *projet* which was submitted to the jury. The architectural language of the *Beaux Arts* was well-established – it was the fully developed apparatus of classicism – and the technology was predominantly traditional, though innovative architects such as Labrouste had successfully introduced cast iron. Kahn, despite his preference for weighty materials (concrete rather than steel, for instance) did not eschew twentieth century technique, but saw it as part of the task of the architect to develop a language for building which would express the nature of the institution in the most direct way. Kahn therefore organised building services carefully, to ensure their subservience, and spoke, poetically, of "asking" the materials he employed how they wanted to be used:

> If you talk to a brick and ask it what it likes it'll say it likes an arch. And you say to it, look arches are expensive and you can always use a concrete lintel to take the place of an arch. And the brick says, I know it's expensive and I'm afraid it cannot be built these days, but if you ask me what I *like* it's still an arch.[62]

Just as in his conceptual design, so in the development of the project towards realisation, the universal nature of a world of forms, or materials, is stressed, over the particularities of the situation. The material has its own desire to return to its origins, as it were, to behave in the way it wants to behave.

Rem Koolhaas

Commentators on the work of the Dutch architect Rem Koolhaas are united in seeing his early career as a film-maker as a key to his architectural position.[63] He had spent his childhood in the Dutch East Indies and intended a career in journalism and film-making, before studying architecture in London at the Architectural Association School. In René Daalder's satirical film *The White Slave* (1969), on the script for which Koolhaas worked, a woman says "listening to this music your brother and I dreamt of a better world". And the answer is: "A better world [...] it has not come to much". Like Koolhaas' architecture, the film is sophisticated, ironic, formally skilful and founded on a bleakly realist philosophy. In 1995, Koolhaas's work to date, through his practice, the Office of Metropolitan Architecture (OMA) was recorded in a volume entitled *S, M, L, XL*, and the projects and essays described therein are used below as the key to understanding Koolhaas's position [Koolhaas, 1995].

被瓦尔特·格罗皮乌斯(Walter Gropius)及其追随者倡导。对他们来说，建筑形式是通过现代科技解决功能问题的结果，它应该是自发产生的；由此产生的方案往往是非对称的，架构也往往是重量较轻的。[61] 而康很重视概念性理念的连续性，这类似于十九世纪学院派(Beaux Arts)建筑师们所采用的流程。这些建筑师为获得罗马大奖展开了备受瞩目的角逐，他们首先提出一份草稿(esquisse)，即代表其主要设计构思的小草图，然后是口袋图（poché），即一叠口袋大小的体现其设计原则的图样，只有在第三阶段才绘制出具体、美观的最终项目图样并提交给评审委员会。学院派的建筑语言已被大家普遍接受，它是得到充分发展的关于古典主义的组织体系，技术也主要是传统型的，但拉布鲁斯特等创新型建筑师成功地引入了铸铁材料。尽管康偏好有重量感的材料（例如混凝土而非钢铁），他并没有摒弃二十世纪的技术，而是将二十世纪的技术看做是建筑师发展建筑语言的任务当中的一部分，这种建筑语言要能够以最直接的方式表达机构的性质。因此康非常认真地开展建造服务，保证服务的从属性，并且颇富诗意地表示，他会"询问"所使用的材料希望以何种方式被使用：

> 如果你与一块砖对话，问它喜欢什么，它会告诉你它喜欢做拱门。你告诉它，拱门是很昂贵的，人们总是用混凝土过梁来取代拱门。砖块回答，我知道拱门很昂贵，我也担心现在不会再建造拱门了，但如果你问我喜欢什么，我仍然会说是拱门。[62]

正如康的概念性设计所体现的，在实现项目的过程中，强调的是形式或者材料的普遍性质，而不是环境的特殊性。材料本身在某种程度上也渴望回归本源，以它想要的方式去呈现。

雷姆·库哈斯

对荷兰建筑师雷姆·库哈斯的建筑作品，评论家们一致认为，他早期作为电影制片人的职业经历是了解其建筑立场的一个关键。[63] 雷姆·库哈斯在荷属东印度群岛度过童年时代，他有意从事新闻业和电影制作，后来赴伦敦建筑联盟学院学习建筑。在库哈斯撰写的由雷尼·达德尔执导的讽刺电影《白人奴隶》（1969）电影脚本中，一位女性说道"听着音乐，你的哥哥和我都梦到了一个更好的世界"。而回答是："更好的世界……还没来到"。正如库哈斯的建筑一样，这部电影是复杂的、讽刺性的，形式精巧，构建在一种阴郁的现实主义哲学的基础上。1995年，库哈斯的作品被由他创立的大都会建筑事务所（OMA）收录到名为《S、M、L、XL》的合辑中。我们用合辑中的项目和文章作为理解库哈斯立场的钥匙[库哈斯，1995]。

S, M, L, XL stands for "small, medium, large, extra-large" – the descriptions used by supermarkets for their undergarments; indeed pictures of men's underpants crop up in the pages of *S, M, L, XL*, which is typographically and visually witty and inventive. One of the theses of the book is that sheer scale (rather than architectural meanings, or the formal ordering devices traditionally used in architectural design) determines the conditions for architecture today. We will treat selected projects, and the issues they raise in the order in which they are published.

Villa Dall'Ava is a house in a suburb of Paris, completed in 1991. The reader is introduced to the brief for the house by means of an apparent film-script. Koolhaas has received a letter from the client requesting a meeting:

> He would pick me up at Charles de Gaulle Airport. When I came out, there was an enormous scandal: someone was trying to kill a policeman.
> It turned out to be him. The policeman had asked him to move, but since he was waiting for his architect he had tried to run over the policeman. [Koolhaas, 1995, p. 133]

Like many of Koolhaas's buildings, Villa Dall'Ava is a commentary on the heroic optimism of the twentieth century, but seen from a melancholic perspective. The house is close to two of Le Corbusier's famous villas. Its ribbon-windowed elevation clearly refers to the *fenêtre en longeur* which constitutes one of Le Corbusier's famous "five points" of the new architecture. But the walls, instead of being formed of a machine-like white render, are made of rust-coloured corrugated metal, and the columns, or *piloti*, are angled, not vertical. The house celebrates the Corbusian "essential joys" and has a swimming pool on the roof, but the white protective pipe railings originally proposed have been removed in favour of orange "temporary" fencing. Le Corbusier had promoted the analogy between steamships and buildings: ships with their decks and promenades, repetitive cabin structures and a general air of purposiveness represented the paradigm of an architecture which would speak its function. In *S, M, L, XL* Koolhaas reproduces draft drawings of Villa Dall'Ava on which he has scribbled in red biro: " I hate the ship metaphor. Railings are very hard to do without resurrecting the ocean liner from the 20's" [Koolhaas, 1995, p. 180]. The completed house is illustrated by photographs presented as if they were stills from a movie, many taken at night. People appear as shadows or reflections; there is a giraffe in the garden.

A 1983 essay reproduced in M, the second section of *S, M, L, XL*, is entitled "Typical Plan" [Koolhaas, 1995, pp. 135-350]. It celebrates "zero-degree architecture, architecture stripped of all traces of uniqueness and specificity". The product of the "new world", "Typical Plan" answers the programmatic needs of business – neutral, artificial, repetitive, an example of utilitarianism "refined as a sensuous science of co-ordination" so that the architecture "transcends the practical to emerge in a rarified existential domain of *pure objectivity*". The Typical Plan "is to the office population what graph paper is to the mathematical curve", but of course it has attracted criticism, especially in Europe: "Suddenly the graph blamed the graph paper for its lack of character. [...] Nietzsche lost out to Sociology 101". The sociology class is shown the alienating effect of modern office life, compared

《S、M、L、XL》意指"小、中、大、超大",这是超市用来描述内衣产品尺寸的说法;的确,男性内裤的图片意外出现在《S、M、L、XL》的页面当中,这在印刷设计和视觉呈现上都是诙谐而别出心裁的。合辑中的一篇文章表明,庞大的规模(而不是建筑的意义,或建筑设计传统上所使用的关于形式次序的方法)决定了当今建筑的状况。我们根据合辑中的发表顺序,对所选择的若干项目及其引发的问题分别进行探讨。

达尔雅瓦别墅是巴黎郊区的一栋住宅,竣工于1991年。合辑运用电影剧本风格的文字向读者简要介绍了这栋住宅。库哈斯收到了一封客户的信要求见面:

> 他会到夏尔戴高乐机场接我。当我出来的时候却听到一个骇人听闻的消息:
> 有人想要谋杀警察。
> 结果发现是他干的。警察要求他把车挪开,但是因为他正在等待他的建筑师,竟想要开车从警察身上轧过去。[库哈斯,1995,第133页]

和库哈斯的许多建筑一样,达尔雅瓦别墅是对二十世纪英雄乐观主义的诠释,但它采用了一个忧郁的视角。这栋别墅距离柯布西耶设计的两栋知名别墅很近。这栋住宅位于高地上的带状窗明显参考了柯布西耶著名的新建筑"五点原则"中的一点,即横向长窗(fenêtre en longeur)。但别墅外墙并没有采用像机器粉刷般的白色底色,而是采用铁锈色的波纹状金属;立柱,或者说底层架空柱,是有角度的,而非垂直的。这栋住宅颂扬了柯布西耶的"本质的快乐",在屋顶上设了一个游泳池,但舍弃了最初设想的白色的、保护性的护栏,取而代之的是橘色的"临时性"栅栏。勒·柯布西耶提倡轮船和建筑之间的类比:带有甲板和走廊的轮船、重复性的舱室结构以及总体氛围的目的性,代表了建筑物的范式,而这种范式体现了建筑的功能所在。《S、M、L、XL》中提供了库哈斯设计达尔雅瓦别墅的草图,草图上有他用伯罗红色圆珠笔书写的潦草字迹:"我讨厌这种轮船的比喻。如果不恢复二十年代的远洋客轮,就很难做栏杆"[库哈斯,1995,第180页]。合辑中展示了这栋住宅竣工后许多类似于电影剧照的照片,很多是在夜间拍摄的。人们在照片里的形象表现为阴影或者映像;花园里还有一只长颈鹿。

《S、M、L、XL》合辑第二部分M中包含了一篇1983年名为"典型方案"的文章[库哈斯,1995,第135-350页],它称颂了"零度的建筑,所有独特性和特异性都被剥离的建筑"。"新世界"的产物"典型方案"满足了实际的商业需求,它是中性的、人为仿造的、重复性的,是功用主义"被改造成一门协调感官科学"的范例,建筑物由此"超越了实际,出现在一个具有纯粹客观性的纯净存在范围里"。典型方案"对于办公室人群来说就像方格纸之于数学曲线",但是它确实也招致了很多批评,特别是在欧洲:"突然之间,图表责备方格纸缺乏特点……尼采输给了社会学101(即社会学导论)"。社会学课堂上展示了现代办公生活带来的异化作用,并拿它与

to the "cottage industries" of old, for which the grids of the office plan provide graphic evidence. Maybe architects should soften and humanise the environment in some way? Koolhaas has no time for such sentimentality: the typical office plan represents *par excellence* the conditions of late capitalism and there is nothing that architects can do about that – attempting to conceal the fact by "humane" design is both futile and fundamentally dishonest. Koolhaas illustrates a version of "Typical Plan" with his competition entry for the Morgan Bank in Amsterdam which ruthlessly imports the benefits as well as the disadvantages of the model: "... abstract office space, its dimensions chosen to enable a maximum number of permutations, introducing, in Holland, unusual (and ultimately unwelcome) depth."

The Congrexpo (Grand Palais) at Lille, is one of Koolhaas's "Large" buildings, completed in 1994, and sitting within an "Extra-large" masterplan for Euralille, for which OMA had been selected as planners in 1989. The scale of the total proposals, as a new city ("the centre of gravity for a virtual community of 50 million Western Europeans") on the periphery of the old city, means that any attempt to relate to the former urban context is doomed. The real context in fact is travel at the scale of the continent, not the city on the perimeter of which Eurolille happens to sit. Koolhaas acknowledges that his proposal to build over the TGV tracks is an investment in symbolism – at an additional cost of between 8 and 10%, but judged by his clients to be worth it [Koolhaas, 1995, p. 1070]. The Congrexpo itself has three components, a 5,000-seat concert hall, a conference centre with three auditoria, and a 20,000 square metre exposition hall. His assembly of the parts is "scandalously simple": they are jammed together on an enormous sloping plane of concrete and under a single unifying roof. The client, Jean-Paul Baietto, director of Euralille, particularly appreciated the skills and approach of Koolhaas and his team. In such a context, the audacity to provide complexity of programme within extreme simplicity (or arbitrariness) of form is precisely what is required: Koolhaas has established "a *dynamique d'enfer*, a dynamic from hell" [Koolhaas, 1995, p. 1208].

Koolhaas goes some way towards explaining his attitude in the following passage from *S, M, L, XL*. All the certainties of architecture no longer prevail, in the conditions of the late twentieth and early twenty-first century city. The previous generation was "making sandcastles. Now we swim in the sea that swept them away." To survive, he writes:

> urbanism will have to imagine a new newness. Liberated from its atavistic duties, urbanism redefined as a way of operating on the inevitable will attack architecture, invade its trenches, drive it from its bastions, undermine its certainties, explode its limits, ridicule its preoccupations with matter and substance, destroy its traditions, smoke out its practitioners. The seeming failure of the urban offers an exceptional opportunity, a pretext for Nietzschean frivolity. We have to imagine 1,001 other concepts of city; we have to take insane risks; we have to dare to be utterly uncritical; we have to swallow deeply and bestow forgiveness left and right. The certainty of failure has to be our laughing gas/oxygen; modernization our most potent drug. Since we are not responsible, we have to become irresponsible. [Koolhaas, 1995]

Koolhaas is not alone in the general bleakness (or realism) of his vision; his work has

旧时代的"家庭手工业"相比较，办公室规划中的格子间为这一观点提供了图形证据。也许建筑师应该在某种程度上使环境变得柔和并且人性化？库哈斯没有时间考虑这种多愁善感：典型的办公室方案代表着晚期资本主义最卓越的环境，建筑师对其无能为力——试图通过"人性化的"设计掩盖事实，既是无用的，从根本上说也是不诚实的。库哈斯拿他为阿姆斯特丹的摩根银行所做的竞赛投标方案来阐释"典型方案"的一个版本，该作品毫不留情地展示了这一模式的优势和劣势："……抽象的办公室空间，选择利用办公室的维度来创造最大数量的排列组合，向荷兰引入了很少见的（最终也是不受欢迎的）纵深度。"

里尔会议展示中心（大皇宫）是库哈斯的"大号"建筑之一，竣工于1994年，隶属于欧洲里尔（Euralille）的"超大型"总体规划，大都会建筑事务所于1989年被选定为项目规划者。全部提案所涉及的规模，即在旧城外围建造一座新城（"五千万西欧人的虚拟社区之重心"），意味着任何试图联系以往城市环境的尝试都是注定要失败的。实际上真正的环境是在欧洲大陆范围内的旅行，而不是欧洲里尔碰巧坐落其中的那座城市。库哈斯承认，他关于在TGV高速列车轨道上盖楼的提议是为了其象征意义所做的一种投资，由此新增的成本在8%到10%之间，但他的客户判断认为这是值得的[库哈斯，1995，第1070页]。里尔会议展示中心本身有三个组成部分：一个容纳五千人的音乐厅，一个有三个礼堂的会议中心，以及一个两万平方米的展览厅。他对这几个部分的组合"简单得令人愕然"：它们在一个巨大的混凝土倾斜平面上紧挨在一起，并且位于同一个屋顶之下。客户，即欧洲里尔项目总指挥让·保罗·拜艾托，格外欣赏库哈斯及其团队的技巧和方式。用形式的极简性（或随意性）去处理项目的复杂性，这种大胆创新恰恰是这种环境下所需要的：库哈斯建立了一种"来自地狱的动力学"[库哈斯，1995，第1208页]。

库哈斯通过《S，M，L，XL》中的一段话从某种程度上阐明了他的态度。在二十世纪晚期和二十一世纪早期的城市环境下，建筑的所有确定性都不再占据优势。上一代人"在堆建沙堡，而现在我们在海里游泳，大海冲走了那些沙堡。"他写道，为了生存：

> 城市主义将不得不想象出一种更新的新鲜感。城市主义从它的原始责任中解放出来，被重新定义为是在无可避免的事物的基础上进行运转的一种方式，它将攻击建筑，侵入建筑的战壕，把它从堡垒里赶出来，瓦解它的确定性，推翻它的限制，冷落它对事物和本质的关注，摧毁它的传统，揭发它的从业者。而城市表面上的失败提供了一个绝佳的机会，为尼采式的轻浮提供了一个借口。我们必须想象关于城市的其他1001种概念；我们必须进行疯狂的冒险；我们必须敢于完全不加批判；我们必须深深地忍耐，并且在各方面给予宽恕。失败的确定性不得不成为让我们欢笑的毒气/氧气；现代化不得不成为我们最有效的药品。因为不是我们的责任，所以我们必须变得不负责任。[库哈斯，1995]

库哈斯在阴郁的（或现实主义的）视角方面并不孤单；他的作品

been influenced by the Dutch writer and artist Armando (Herman Dirk van Dodeweerd), and the author Willem Frederik Hermans (1921-1995). Armando writes:

> Do not take morality or interpretation of reality as your starting point, but emphasise the given. Accept reality as it is in any way [...] result: Authenticity! The artist is no longer artist but the cold rational eye. [Armando, 1964]

It is clear Koolhaas's approach has much in common with the "Dionysian" aspect of Nietzsche's philosophy. But there are also aspects of "Apollonian" Nietzscheism in his work – the surreal empty photographs of some of the spaces in the Villa Dall'Avra, and his "House for Two Friends" of 1988. Koolhaas's belief that it is irresponsible not to acknowledge the brutal conditions of modernity is everywhere apparent; we have no choice but to despair at the condition of architecture, though in the hands of a hero there is an opportunity for sublimating an ironic or hyperenergetic response into something that might approach poetry.

Alvar Aalto

The work of the Finnish architect Alvar Aalto, and in particular his building known as Baker House, is selected to illustrate a pragmatic, or synthetic approach. Baker House is a dormitory for the Massachusetts Institute of Technology, designed in 1946 while Aalto held a visiting professorship there. The site runs along the north side of the Charles River and from the very start Aalto's plans seek to find ways of maximising the view of the river for every student. Early sketches show clusters of rooms facing south, and because a simple single-sided slab would not contain sufficient rooms, several ways are examined of increasing the density: by parallel blocks in echelon, by fan-shaped ends, and by the "giant gentle polygon", resolving itself into a sinuous curve, that was finally adopted. This gives a wide variety of room shapes, with the advantage that most rooms look along the river east or west rather than just straight across it. His presentation to the building committee post-rationalised the final form by comparing it to still more possible patterns, parallel blocks at right angles to the river, for example, which might be efficient but fail to take advantage of the site. As in so many examples of Aalto's work, the formal solution is intuitive, only achieved after many free-hand sketched alternatives, some of which might seem inherently implausible, but the design, once reached, is then subject to scrutiny in quite measurable ways. A single-loaded corridor was undoubtedly more expensive than a regular central corridor arrangement with rooms both sides, but provided Aalto could achieve a cost per bed-space of $5,300 it could be justified.

Baker House reflects many of Aalto's social convictions and formal strategies. Firstly, the sets of rooms can be seen as an illustration of what Aalto might mean by his call for "flexible standardisation". Each cell is essentially identical, but because of the shaped curve on plan 22 different room shapes are created on a typical floor of 43 rooms. This meant numerous special details, for the built-in furniture in each room for example, but

受到了荷兰作家和艺术家阿曼多（赫尔曼•德尔克•范•都德维尔德）以及作家威廉•弗雷德里克•赫尔曼（1921-1995）的影响；阿曼多曾写道：

> 不要把道德或者对现实的解读作为你的出发点，而要强调既定的事实。全然接受现实的本来面目……结果是：真实性！艺术家不再是艺术家，而是冷静而理性的眼睛。[阿曼多，1964]

很明显，库哈斯的方式和尼采哲学的"酒神精神"有很多共通之处。但他的作品中也有着尼采学说"日神精神"的一些元素——包括关于达尔雅瓦别墅中某些空间的超现实的、空荡荡的照片，以及1988年他"为两个朋友设计的住宅"。库哈斯认为，若不承认现代性的恶劣环境这一观点，将是不负责任的；我们别无选择，唯有对建筑的环境感到绝望，尽管我们对此做出的一个讽刺性或者超有力的回应，在英雄的手中还有机会升华成有望接近于诗歌的东西。

阿尔瓦•阿尔托

我们选择了芬兰建筑师阿尔瓦•阿尔托的作品，特别是他设计的有贝克楼之称的建筑，来说明一种务实性的或综合性的方式。贝克楼是麻省理工学院的宿舍楼，设计于1946年，当时阿尔托在该校担任访问教授。宿舍楼地处查尔斯河的北岸。从一开始，阿尔托的方案就在寻找一些途径以便让每个学生都尽可能地欣赏到水景。早期的草图显示有很多朝南的房间，仅有一面的板楼无法容纳足够多的房间，因此他考察了若干种提升密度的方法：包括排成梯形的平行建筑物、呈扇形的尾端、以及"角度柔和的巨型多边形"，使得整个设计成为一条蜿蜒的曲线，这种方式最终被采纳。这使得房间形状有了很多种变化，其好处是大多数房间都能够欣赏到查尔斯河的西面或东面，而不仅仅是望向河对岸。事后，他在给建造委员会的陈述中对最终的形式做了合理化解释，把它与其它当时看来更可行的方式进行对比，例如与河垂直的互相平行的楼房，这种设计可能是高效的，但并不能充分发挥地理位置的优势。在诸多的阿尔托建筑作品范例中，形式的解决方案是凭直觉获得的，只是基于许多随心所欲的手绘图选择方案而确定的，其中一些也许看似根本不可能，但设计一旦成型，就能够经受住测量方式的检验。单侧式走廊无疑比常规的两侧有房间中间设走廊的建造成本更高，但只要阿尔托能够把每张床位空间的成本控制在$5300美元，这种设计就是合理的。

贝克楼反映了阿尔托的很多社会理念和形式策略。首先，阿尔托倡导"灵活的标准化"，这些房间能够诠释他这一观点可能具有的内涵。每一个房间都是相同的，但由于规划中的蜿蜒曲线，在一个包含43间房间的普通楼层里有22种不同的房间形状。这意味着不计其数的别致的细节，例如每间房的嵌入式家具，但

from a basically similar vocabulary. The general notion of the wave-form seems like a huge enlargement of the experimental wood sculptures, on which Aalto had been engaged with Otto Korhonen since the late 1920s, or a recapitulation on the urban scale of the 1938 New York Fair interior, his only previous work in the United States. Aalto built the free form of the rooms in a "rustic" brick — indeed he went to particular lengths to find dark red bricks that were rough-textured and included clinkers — but clad the orthogonal main common room in limestone. It is treated as a calm and static space, in contrast to the dynamic of the climbing stairs.

During the same period, Walter Gropius, with his Cambridge-based practice TAC, was building a group of student residences off Harvard Yard to a similar brief. Though it did not have the benefit of the Charles River bordering it, the site is a challenging one, at the end of a sequence of open courts formed by buildings by architects of the stature of H.H. Richardson and McKim Mead and White. Gropius fails to do justice to either the potential of the programme or the opportunities of the site. Gropius seems to subscribe to a positivistic attitude to function in that he answers every measurable problem, but then allows himself some relaxation in a bit of whimsy. But his definition of the functional was not wide enough. A reductive modernist approach, which accepts without demur the economics of the double-sided corridor, leads to a series of similar blocks which, however, are disposed without regard to orientation. Their form is "softened" in the expression of the service areas, by projecting them slightly and sometimes angling their flank walls. Despite the pleasant well-treed spaces the intended picturesque effect is weak and the articulation of the buildings by distinguishing the bathrooms less convincing than Aalto's stress on the special character of the common areas. In fact, by addressing more completely understood programmatic issues (such as the provision of spaces for internal meeting) directly, Aalto succeeds in inventing a surprisingly powerful form. The requirement, for security reasons, for a single main entrance, leads to the dramatic and apparently unprecedented pair of cantilevered staircases which rise up from a first floor landing over the central entrance, and create what appears from the distance to be a giant inverted pediment. These great naturally-lit stairs perform a social function, because instead of rigorously separating the "social" areas from the areas devoted to circulation, Aalto acknowledges the social function of a staircase and its landings by providing widened areas to allow for informal meetings and conversation; each is differently sized because of the differing positions reached on the long straight flight. The diagonal placing of the limestone-clad ground floor social space might at first sight be taken for a merely formal gesture, until the immediate context is examined. It is accounted for by the angle of the pre-existing approach path from the rest of the campus, which slices right through the block at ground floor level and ends in the double-height dining area.

In contrast to the behaviour of Louis Kahn, in starting with an ideal form which is then modified by circumstances to fit issues of programme, site and budgetary constraint, Aalto's procedure is to begin with precisely those particularities. But the forms that appear to have arrived intuitively in Aalto's imagination were such that they performed well when subjected to testing under a wide range of measurable criteria. If their generation was

都来自一个基本相似的范畴。波浪形的整体概念看起来像是他试验性木雕作品的巨型放大版，他与手工家具生产商奥托•克霍宁自二十世纪二十年代晚期开始合作进行这种木雕试验；波浪形的整体概念又像是对他1938年纽约世界博览会展厅内部城市地域的再现，后者是他此前在美国的唯一作品。阿尔托用"质朴"的砖块构建房间的自由形式——他确实竭尽全力去寻找暗红色的纹理粗糙的砖块，包括渣砖——但是为那呈直角的大公共休息室覆上了石灰岩。这间休息室被塑造成冷静的、静止的空间，和拾阶而上的楼梯的动态形成对比。

在同一时期，瓦尔特•格罗皮乌斯及其位于剑桥的建筑师合作协会（TAC），也正承担着类似的职责，在哈佛园外建造一组学生宿舍。宿舍的选址虽然没有邻近查尔斯河这样的优势，但也很有挑战性，H. H. 理查德森和麦金米德怀特事务所等高水平的建筑师们所设计的大楼形成了一系列的露天庭院，宿舍选址位于其末端。格罗皮乌斯没有能够充分发挥该项目的潜力或利用其选址带来的机遇。他似乎关于功能持一种实证主义的态度，他回答了每一个测量性的问题，但之后又允许自己有一些放松，融入一点异想天开的元素。但他对于功能性的定义不够宽泛。一种简单还原性的现代主义方式毫不犹豫地接受了经济型的双侧式走廊，由此产生了一系列相似的建筑，但这些建筑的处理并未考虑朝向问题。这种形式借助服务区域的呈现方式而得到了"软化"，这些服务区域采取了轻柔的设计，有时它们的侧面墙会形成一些角度。尽管有着令人愉悦的绿树成荫的空间，所设想的如画美效果仍是微弱的，通过不同的浴室来表达建筑物的特征也不如阿尔托对公共区域特征的强化手法那么有说服力。实际上，阿尔托以直截了当的方式去处理浅显易懂的规划性问题（例如为一个内部会议提供空间），由此成功地创造了一个极富力量的形式。鉴于安全原因要求只设一个主要入口，由此诞生了一对戏剧化的、显然并无先例的悬挑楼梯，两个楼梯自一楼向上耸立，坐落于中心入口之上，从远处看起来像是一个巨大的倒三角形。这些出色的有自然光照射的楼梯承担着一种社交功能，因为它并没有将"社交"区域与流动区域严格地分割开来，阿尔托实现了楼梯通道和楼梯口的社交功能，他加宽了这些区域，从而让人们可以进行非正式的会议或交谈；每一个区域大小各异，因为它们与长而直的楼梯的连接位置都是不同的。位于底层的以石灰岩覆盖的社交空间呈斜对角放置，乍一看不过是一种形式方面的姿态，直到你对周遭的环境进行考查。它照顾到了先前已存在的从校园其他地方延展而来的道路的角度，这条路正好穿过建筑物的底层，在两层高的餐饮区域结束。

路易斯•康的做法是，以一种理想的形式开始，然后根据环境条件去修正这种形式，以解决项目、选址和预算限制等方面的问题；阿尔托则与此相反，他恰恰是从特殊性入手的。不过，似乎那些凭直觉进入阿尔托想象中的形式，在根据各种测量标准进行的测试中也表现得很优异。如果说他们那一代

not "rational", they could be shown to be neither wilful nor arbitrary, unlike the signature forms of some "artist" architects of a later generation.

Aalto was in fact sceptical that architecture was an art at all, and according to his biographer Göran Schildt believed the art of building was an art only in the sense that medicine and cooking were arts. He conceived it as a humanistic activity based on technical knowledge which can only be pursued by people with a capacity for creative synthesis.[64]

This attitude provides a way of explaining Aalto's constant pre-occupation with the specifics, of site and context, of materials, and of the study of the poetics of particular functions like washing one's hands or reading a book. It would also account for his well-known scepticism about the mathematics of modular co-ordination: there was nothing special in mathematics except its usefulness. Politically, Aalto's distancing himself from all systems of belief could be seen in the same light. If Aalto was no idealist, it is also clear that he did not subscribe to Nietzschean despair. While Aalto may have shared Nietzsche's view of the preeminence of the artist in society, his concern for everyday comfort and convenience (for "the little man" as he used to describe it) hardly squares with that philosophy. Aalto was closer to an alternative, more optimistic, version of Nominalism, that we described above as "sceptical idealism", which holds that though aesthetic structures are not mimetic of an ideal world, they can assist in improvements: meanings which used to be supported by a symbolic language relating to a "higher order" can to some extent be re-established as an allegory. Aalto described himself as a "positive sceptic" and outlined his position in an address to the Jyväskyla Lycée in 1958:

> The much-discussed sceptical world view is in reality a necessary condition for anyone who would like to make a cultural contribution. This is of course dependent on scepticism's transformation into a positive phenomenon, an unwillingness to 'move with the stream'.
> On a higher level scepticism is transformed into its apparent opposite, to love with a critical sensibility. It is a love that lasts, as it rests on a critically tested foundation. It can result in such a love for the little man that it functions as a kind of guardian when our era's mechanized life style threatens to strangle the individual and the organically harmonious life. [Schildt, 1998, pp. 15-17; Ray, 2005a, p. 187]

Thus for Aalto art was not the imitation of transcendental structures, nor their despairing rejection, but the affirmation that human constructions are none the less real for being merely human. Art becomes (among other things) the affirmation of aspirations that are utopian but secular. As a pragmatic architect, Aalto knew that buildings only got built by the tricky political processes, at which he was adept, of charming his clients and influencing local officials. They were realised using the technologies that were available and in the face of the hard facts of climatic conditions and budgetary constraints. But a building was not just the solution to a mechanical set of problems: an act of invention was required, and sometimes the practice of building could result in an artifact that others would recognise as architecture.

不是"理性的"，他们表现出来的可以说也不是任性的或武断的，和后来的一些"艺术家"建筑师们的标志性形式不同。

实际上，阿尔托对建筑作为一种艺术是持怀疑态度的，他的传记作家格兰•希尔特写道，阿尔托认为，如果建筑艺术是一门艺术的话，那么医学和烹调也是艺术。他将建筑看作是一种基于技术知识的人文主义活动，只有那些有能力创新整合的人们才能够开展这项活动。[64]

上述态度在一定程度上解释了为什么阿尔托总是首先关注特殊性，包括选址和环境的特殊性、材料的特殊性、以及对特定功能如洗手或读书的诗意研究。这也解释了他对于模数协调数学的知名的怀疑论：数学除了它的有用性之外别无所长。这同样也解释了为什么在政治上阿尔托与所有的信条体制保持距离。如果说阿尔托不是一位理想主义者，很显然他同样也不赞同尼采的绝望论。尽管阿尔托可能同意尼采关于艺术家在社会中的卓越性这一观点，但他对于日常舒适性和便利性（他用"小个子"来称呼它们）的关注跟这种哲学几乎是不相符的。阿尔托更接近于唯名论的一个非传统的、更乐观的版本，我们在上文称之为"怀疑型理想主义"，认为尽管美学架构不能模拟理想世界，但还是能够促成改善：过去与"更高的秩序"有关的象征性语言，其包含的意义在某种程度上得以被重新构建为一个寓言。阿尔托形容自己是"积极的怀疑论者"，并在1958年在于韦斯屈莱公立学校的演讲中表述了自己的立场：

> 人们所热议的怀疑主义世界观，实际上对于任何想要做出文化贡献的人们来说都是一个必备条件。当然，这取决于是否能够把怀疑主义转化为一种积极的现象，以及一种不愿"随波逐流"的意愿。
> 在更高的层次上，怀疑主义转向了它的对立面，即以带有批判性的感知能力去爱。这种爱是持久的，因为它立足于一个经受了严酷考验的基础之上。它能够引发对"小个子"的深切的爱，以致于当我们这个时代的机械化生活方式威胁要扼杀个体和有机和谐的生活时，它能够担当起类似于守护者的角色。［希尔特，1998，第15-17页；雷，2005a，第187页］

因此，对阿尔托而言，艺术不是对先验结构的仿效，也不是对这些结构的绝望的摒弃，而是一种肯定，肯定人类建筑依然真实地彰显了人性。艺术肯定了人们那些既乌托邦又世俗化的愿望（艺术的诸多作用之一）。作为一名务实的建筑师，阿尔托知道建筑物的落成必须借助于微妙的政治程序，包括吸引客户并影响当地官员，他在这方面很娴熟。建筑物变为现实都有赖于现有的技术，并且面临着气候条件和预算制约等客观事实。但是，一栋建筑物并不仅仅是对一系列机械问题的解决：其中必须有创新行为，这样有时候建造活动产生的作品才会被他人认可，称之为建筑（architecture）。

Concluding remarks

The reader who has followed us thus far is likely to have encountered more questions than answers. Philosophy has certainly influenced architecture in many ways –and there are even more ways to look philosophically at architecture. In relation to ethics, we concluded that a normative theory that could account for the diverse nature of the discipline of architecture is still difficult to imagine. The culmination of the discussion on Aesthetics suggested that contemplating the problems of architecture, so far from assisting in clarifying philosophical problems, seemed only to reveal them. The positions evident in the three case studies suggest that practising architects do indeed think in very different ways about their discipline, but even if their thought reflects the principles they have absorbed in reading, as well as lessons from practice itself, that does not appear to resolve the many issues we have raised.

If we have succeeded in illustrating the way in which the discipline of architecture focuses on philosophical problems in a particularly acute way, that may serve part of our purpose. But it would be disappointing if that is all that has been achieved. More positively we could claim that this essay has concentrated on the description of ways in which 'thinking' shapes our 'building'. Thinking, (by which we mean philosophy) also helps to understand architecture better by providing theories and categories by which we can conceptualise and analyse architectural phenomena. Architectural forms do not come randomly: how we build is in many ways a response to different or even opposed philosophical approaches.

The different philosophical approaches – actual, or culturally determined – are heterogeneous and sometimes even opposed to each other on the fundamental level of theory. One could take one side in this debate – adopt a positivist position, for example, and suggest that all the unknowables will eventually become measurable, and therefore the apparently deeper problems will go away. One can say that we only need to be true to the phenomena, as phenomenologists do, though that may be at the expense of the respect that we consider due to the advance of science *per se*. In the face of the brutal facts of an unequal world apparently hurtling towards ecological disaster, a melancholic realism is compelling to others. It is the measure of the philosophical nature of these conflicting positions that none of them can be shown to be absolutely false – at any rate if they were proved or disproved they would cease to be philosophical. The acceptance of the many unsolved tensions that philosophy of architecture faces, on the other hand, may lead to a positive view of the position of architecture, which maintains an element of idealism, as follows.

结束语

　　到现在为止一直追随我们的读者们可能遇到的问题比得到的答案还要多。哲学的确能够通过很多方式影响建筑，从哲学角度去看待建筑的方式甚至更多。关于伦理学，我们总结道，仍旧难以想象有一种规范性的理论能够阐释建筑学科的多样性。美学探讨的最终结果表明，对建筑问题的思考非但没有帮忙阐明哲学问题，反而似乎只是揭示了这些问题。三个案例研究显示出的立场，表明执业建筑师们确实在以截然不同的方式思考着他们的学科，然而，即使他们的想法反映了他们从阅读中吸收的原则以及从实践中取得的经验，其想法似乎并没有解决我们提出的很多问题。

　　如果我们已经成功地说明了建筑学科是如何以一种极其敏锐的方式聚焦于哲学问题的，这可能就达到了我们的一部分目的。但是如果这就是我们取得的全部成就，那是很令人失望的。从更积极的方面来看，我们可以说这篇文章集中描写了"思考"是以哪些方式来塑造我们的"建筑物"的。思考（我们指的是哲学）还有助于我们更好地理解建筑，因为它提供了理论和范畴，让我们能够把建筑学现象概念化并展开分析。建筑形式并不是偶然出现的：我们的建造方式在很多方面是对各种不同的甚至相反的哲学方法的回应。

　　不同的哲学方法——不管是基于实际层面的还是文化层面的——多种多样，它们有时甚至在基本理论层面上都是彼此冲突的。人们在这场辩论中可以选择某一方的立场——比如采纳实证主义的立场，认为所有不可知的因素最终都是可测量的，更深层次的问题也就消失不见了。人们可以说，我们只需要忠于现象，正如现象学家所做的那样，　但这可能是以牺牲了科学进步本身所应得的尊重为代价的。面对一个显然在向着生态灾难的方向飞驰而去的不公平世界这一严酷事实，有人会发现忧郁的现实主义更有说服力。正是因为考量了这些彼此冲突的立场背后的哲学本质，所以没有哪个立场能被证明是完全错误的——无论如何，如果这些立场被证实或者被驳倒，那它们就不再具有哲学性了。在另一方面，接受建筑哲学所面临的许多悬而未决的冲突，也可能引发关于建筑立场的具有积极意义的观点，这种积极观点一直是理想主义的一个要素，如下所述。

Architecture itself can be regarded as a way of overcoming philosophical tensions by suggesting practical possibilities, namely designs, that appear to bridge between rival theories and approaches. Design is in fact the core human discipline, being the only activity that properly involves the imaginative conception of ideas, leading to artifacts that are realised as actual constructions in the world. Thus architects are, uniquely, in a position to fashion buildings and spaces that, at least in the interpretation of some, can offer resolutions to the dichotomies and tensions that are endemic to philosophy.

建筑本身可以被看作是一种超越哲学冲突的路径，它通过提供实际的可行性方案，即设计，在彼此对立的理论和方法之间搭建起了一座桥梁。设计实际上是最核心的人类行为，是唯一一种恰当地对理念进行充满想象力的创造的活动，由此产生的作品是世界上真实的建筑物。因此，建筑师能够以独特的方式塑造建筑物和空间，至少按照某些人的解读，这些建筑物和空间能够为哲学所特有的二分法和冲突提供解决方案。

[1] The city, rather than architecture *per se*, has been a fruitful area for philosophical reflection, from Jerusalem as a metaphor through St Augustine, and from Plato's *polis* to the writings of Derrida, Habermas and Alexander Mitscherlich. But it would not be possible to do justice to this topic in a small book. For the complex issues raised by cities see Meagher [2008].

[2] Most commentators regard Vitruvius as a muddled thinker, whose writings are an eclectic collection of the work of others. Nevertheless he had a concern for practical inventiveness, and a profound respect for traditions that had been inherited from the Greeks. His convoluted prose is the despair of modern translators, just as it was for Alberti in the Renaissance, who even suggested at one time that it would have been better if his *Ten Books* had never survived. See [Vitruvius. 2001].

[3] As William Lethaby (1857-1931) put it: "a Gothic cathedral may be compared to a great cargo-ship which has to attain to a balance between speed and safety. The church and the ship were both designed in the same way by a slow perfecting of parts; all was effort acting on custom, beauty was mastery, fitness, size with economy of material." [Lethaby, 1955, p. 158]. Historians have answered by indicating the highly self-conscious ways in which Gothic architecture developed stylistically. See [Panofsky, 1957].

[4] The emphasis is characteristic of this book, which had a powerful influence as propaganda.

[5] And such reflection can be seen as an essential component of responsible "practice". See also [Schön, 1983].

[6] See for example "Bauen für Despoten?" in *Der Spiegel Spezial*, Nr.4, S. 84-87, 2002.

[7] For a brief introduction to Aalto's life and work see Ray [2005].

[8] For a detailed discussion of this issue see [Watkin, 1977]. An earlier refutation occurs in [Scott, 1980].

[9] http://www.katarxis3.com/Alexander_Eisenman_Debate.htm (23.3.2008).

[10] Of course there is the danger of what has been called an "intentional fallacy". Even if architects intend certain meanings, these might not be evident in the actual design. See [Wimsatt and Beardsley, 1954].

[11] See [Forty, 2000].

[12] For the different meanings of nature see [Lovejoy, 1927].

[13] It is a mistake to see Alberti's thinking as purely Platonic or Neo-Platonic, however: his theory incorporates aspects of Aristotelian thinking, and as Erwin Panofsky points out, his definition of beauty "renounces any metaphysical explanation of the beautiful". See [Panofsky, 1968].

[14] Le Corbusier did not follow Alberti's prescriptions in relation to religious architecture, however: his pilgrimage church at Ronchamp used a complex free form, whereas in *Vers une Architecture* he illustrates simple housing schemes based on a pure cube. In the nineteenth century the ideas of *gestalt* psychology had provided a further argument for pure geometries: they could be perceived more easily and were thus "stronger" figures.

[15] In particular Rudolf Wittkower. This interpretation of Alberti's theory of the colonnade and wall follows that advocated in his *Architectural Principles in the Age of Humanism*, of 1949. Others have argued that Alberti never refers to contemporary buildings, so that the principles he advocates are not to be understood as prescriptions. His book is certainly not a "primer" for use by practitioners, in the way that the later treatise by Sebastiano Serlio was. See [Kruft, 1994].

[16] For this meaning of Historicism see [Meinecke, 1946]. A good discussion of the history of the term can be found in [Mandelbaum, 1967, IV, 22-25].

[17] It is obvious that much of this anticipates Sigmund Freud's suggestion that the irrational and libido-driven subconscious is decisive for human actions, especially as a prime source of artistic production. Yet for Freud it is mainly the *sublimation* of primitive instincts that finds its outlet in human creativity, not the direct expression of the libidinous impulse. A second difference is that for Freud the subconscious is a possible object of science since it follows rules and principles that are universal to all mankind and that can be discovered empirically. (That is why *Traumdeutung* can be a scientific endeavour.)

[18] See [Kruft, 1994].

[19] Charles Jencks' *Le Corbusier and the Tragic View of Architecture* makes a case that Nietzsche is fundamental to Le Corbusier's thinking.

[20] A distinction should be made between different notions of reason, which it has been suggested

¹ 对于城市（而非建筑之类）的哲学反思可谓是著作丰厚，从圣·奥古斯汀对耶路撒冷的隐喻、柏拉图的城邦论，到德里达、哈贝马斯以及亚历山大·米切利希的著作，不一而足。但是我们无法通过一本小书对这个题目展开充分讨论。与城市有关的复杂问题，参见马尔(2008)。

² 多数评论家认为维特鲁威是个思绪混乱的思想家，其著作是对他人作品的兼收并蓄。不过，他关注实际的创造力，而且对从希腊人那里传承下来的传统深怀敬意。维特鲁威晦涩的文字令文艺复兴时代的阿尔伯蒂感到绝望，同样地令现代译者绝望。阿尔伯蒂甚至一度认为，如果维特鲁威的《建筑十书》没有留存下来会更好一些。参见[维特鲁威，2001]。

³ 正如威廉·莱瑟比(1857－1931)所言："一座哥特式大教堂或许可以和一个必须在速度与安全之间达到平衡的大货船相提并论。教堂和船舶以同样的方式设计而成，即各部件的渐趋完善，一切都是根据惯例做出的努力，美是掌控，是恰如其分，是节俭用料而形成的规模。"（莱瑟比，1955，158页）。历史学家们指出了哥特式建筑在其风格发展过程中的高度自觉的方式。参见[潘诺夫斯基，1957]。

⁴ 引文中的重点是原著所标注的，有力地强化了其宣传效果。

⁵ 正如我们要在下文探讨的，这种反思可以说是负责任的"实践"的一个重要组成部分。亦可参见[绍恩，1983]。

⁶ 参见Der Spiegel Spezial, Nr.4, S. 84-87, 2002 关于 "Bauen für Despoten?" 的范例。

⁷ 关于阿尔托生平和作品的简要介绍，参见雷[2005]。

⁸ 关于这一问题的详细讨论，参见[沃特金，1977]。更早的批判出现在[斯科特，1980]。

⁹ http://www.katarxis3.com/Alexander_Eisenman_Debate.htm (23.3.2008)。

¹⁰ 当然也存在所谓"意图谬误"的危险。即使建筑师意图体现某种意义，但在实际设计中体现得并不明显，见[维姆萨特与比尔兹利，1954].

¹¹ 见[福蒂，2000]。

¹² 要了解本质的不同意义，见[洛夫乔伊，1927]。

¹³ 但是，不能错误地把阿尔伯蒂的思想看做是纯柏拉图主义或纯新柏拉图主义的：他的理论融合了亚里士多德思想的某些方面，并且，正如欧文·潘诺夫斯基指出的，阿尔伯蒂对美的定义"抛弃了对美好事物的一切形而上的解释"。见[潘诺夫斯基,1968]

¹⁴ 然而，勒·柯布西耶并未遵从阿尔伯蒂关于宗教建筑的训示：他的郎香朝圣教堂采用了一种复杂而自由的形式，而在《走向新建筑》中他却展示了以纯粹的立方体为基础的简约房屋建筑方案。19世纪的格式塔心理学理论关于纯粹的几何图形做了更进一步的论述：这些图形更容易被理解，因此是"更有力"的图形。

¹⁵ 特别是鲁道夫·维特科夫尔。对阿尔伯蒂关于列柱和墙理论的解读遵循了鲁道夫·维特科夫尔在《人文主义时代的建筑原则》（1949）一书中所倡导的观点。其他人则认为阿尔伯蒂从未提及现代建筑物，因此维特科夫尔所倡导的原则并不能作为解读阿尔贝蒂的有效方法。维特科夫尔的著作对从业人员来说显然并不能像塞巴斯蒂安·塞里欧的专著一样作为"入门书籍"使用。见[克鲁夫特，1994]

¹⁶ 关于历史主义的这一含义，参见[迈纳克,1946]。[曼德尔鲍姆，1967，IV，22-25]对这一术语的历史进行了充分探讨。

¹⁷ 很明显，这里预见了西格蒙德·弗洛伊德的看法，即非理性的、性欲推动的潜意识对人的行为是决定性的，特别是作为艺术作品的主要来源。但对于弗洛伊德而言，原始本能在人类创造力方面找到了升华的出口，而不是直接表现为性欲冲动。第二个区别是对于弗洛伊德而言，潜意识是一个可能的科学研究对象，因为潜意识遵循的规律和法则普适于全人类，并且可由实证发现。（这是梦的解析成为科学研究的原因。）

¹⁸ 见[克鲁夫特，1994]。

¹⁹ 查尔斯·詹克斯《勒·柯布西耶和悲剧建筑观》论证了尼采对勒·柯布西耶的思想形成非常重要。

²⁰ 我们应该区分关于理性的不同概念，研究表明，

Heidegger does not acknowledge sufficiently in his readings of Western philosophy. His critique is directed against what has sometimes been called instrumental reason, but it leaves out richer notions of reason, like Kant's *Vernunft*, that are able to identify ends as much as means.

[21] These remarks by Heidegger are from a 1929-1930 lecture course, cited in [Wigley, 1992].

[22] For a more extended discussion of this influence see the excellent article by Woessner [2003].

[23] See this remark: "The flight into tradition, out of a combination of humility and presumption, can bring about nothing in itself other than self-deception and blindness in relation to the historical moment", in "The Age of the World Picture" [Heidegger, 1938].

[24] See [Woessner, 2003].

[25] Since the details of the "Heidegger case" became widely known in 1987, his involvement with Nazism has been much discussed. It remains an open question to what extent his philosophical ideas and insights are discredited thereby. It is also a point of debate, whether his architectural philosophy has been shaped by the *Blut* and *Boden* ideology of the Third Reich. This influence has been argued for by Doreen Massey [1994] amongst others, while Julian Young [2002], for example, pleads for an independence of Heidegger's philosophy; he sees it as uncompromised by his political involvement. Yet whether or not there is a link between his ideas and Nazi-ideology, his architectural philosophy is certainly detachable from any such alleged connection: all those who developed Heidegger's ideas of dwelling further, have done so without any link to Nazism.

[26] Which he would not call "metaphysics".

[27] Radio interview quoted in [Games, 1985, p. 31].

[28] This is an epistemological problem of which naïve postmodernist authors seem be unaware.

[29] In order to function as a building, however, any Post-Modern architecture requires technical knowledge and is based upon the (at least implicit) trust that this knowledge is universally applicable. And the search for an architecture that *expresses* the diversity and ambiguity of the world seems to suggest some universal normative ideal – namely that art should be an expression of the way things are (in the Post-Modern argument, diverse and contradictory).

[30] This is one way of seeing Le Corbusier's buildings at Chandigarh, described above. Few can be found to defend Le Corbusier's city plans, but Venturi in fact admires the complexity and inherent contradictions of Le Corbusier's architecture: it is naïve and unskilful modernism that he is chiefly concerned to attack.

[31] This part is partly based upon (and takes material from) [Illies, 2008].

[32] See also [Spector, 2005].

[33] See www.galinsky.com/buildings/vitraf.

[34] Data from the U.S. Department of Energy (http://www.eartheasy.com/article_global_warming.htm, 23.3.2008).

[35] http://www.unep.or.jp/ietc/focus/EnergyCities1 .asp See also [Fox, 2000; Williamson and Radford, 2000].

[36] Obviously, the effects on human behaviour are often very close to the effects on psychological well-being: Whether people are happy or unhappy will influence what they are likely to do; it might have been the cold and impersonal effect of some modern social housing project that has encouraged vandalism.

[37] See [Posener, 1978, p. 164].

[38] For a general overview see Mikellides, http://bejlt.brookes.ac.uk/article/architectural_psychology_19692007/.

[39] http://www.defensiblespace.com/start.htm. and Newman [1973]. It should be added that the well-documented physical and mental illnesses associated with poorly designed social housing projects are often caused primarily by economic and social deprivation, the impoverished quality of the architecture merely illustrating the problem and inevitably compounding it.

[40] For an extended discussion of this and other examples see [Leach, 1999].

[41] Only if one understands ethics in a wider sense, would all of this be covered by such a methodology; it would need to achieve an overall balance between such different requirements as sustainability, effi-

海德格尔在对西方哲学进行解读时并未充分考虑这一点。他的批判针对的是有时可称做工具主义理性的概念，而忽略了更丰富的理性概念，例如康德的"纯粹理性"。康德认为，理性不仅能提供一种技术层面的认知，而且他宣称价值也可以用理性的方式去讨论。

21 海德格尔的这些说法来自于1929年至1930年之间的演讲课，[威格利，1992]有提及。

22 如果要对这种影响力做更进一步的探讨，参见渥斯纳[2003]的精彩文章。

23 见以下评论："以谦卑而充满预设的方式投身于传统，带来的只能是关于历史性时刻的自欺欺人和盲目无知"，《世界图景年代》[海德格尔，1938]。

24 见[渥斯纳，2003]。

25 自从"海德格尔案"的细节在1987年变得广为人知，他卷入纳粹党一事便引发诸多讨论。这在多大程度上损害了他的哲学观点和见解的公信力，仍然是一个悬而未决的问题。另外一个争论的焦点是，他的建筑哲学是否由第三帝国的"血和土"的意识形态所塑造。朵林·马西[1994]等人认为他的哲学受到了纳粹的影响，而朱利安·杨[2002]等人则为其哲学的独立性辩护；他认为海德格尔哲学并没有受到其政治立场的影响。不管海德格尔的观点和纳粹意识形态之间是否存在关联，他的建筑哲学肯定没有受到前两者之间关系的影响；所有那些进一步发展了海德格尔栖居理念的人们，都是在与纳粹无任何关联的情况下做到这一点的。

26 他不会称其为"形而上学"。

27 [格姆斯，1985，p. 31]中引用了电台采访。

28 这是幼稚的后现代主义作者们似乎尚未觉察到的认知论问题。

29 然而，为了具备建筑的功能，任何后现代建筑都需要技术知识，并且相信（至少是暗自相信）这些技术知识是普世适用的。人们在寻求一种建筑来表达世界的多样性和模糊性，这似乎指向了一种普世的、规范性的理想，即艺术应该是事物存在方式的表达（在后现代的观点里，事物的存在是多样化且相互矛盾的）。

30 这是看待上文所述的勒·柯布西耶在昌迪加尔所设计建筑的一种方式。很少有人为柯布西耶的城市方案辩护，但事实上文丘里对柯布西耶的建筑的复杂性和内在矛盾性相当赞赏：他主要攻击的是幼稚而笨拙的现代主义。

31 本章节的部分依据来自[伊利斯，2008]（并从中获取了一些素材）。

32 也见[斯佩克特，2005]。

33 http://www.galinsky.com/buildings/vitraf。

34 数据来源于美国能源部（http://www.eartheasy.com/article_global_warming.htm, 23.3.2008）。

35 http://www.unep.or.jp/ietc/focus/EnergyCities1.asp。也可参见[福克斯，2000；威廉姆森和拉德福，2000]。

36 参见[波泽纳，1978，p. 164]。

37 很显然，对人类行为的影响通常几乎等同于对人类心理状态的影响：人们开心与否将影响到他们接下来的行为；一些现代公租房项目给人们带来冰冷、没有人情味的效果，有可能激发蓄意破坏行为。

38 关于总体概述，见麦克莱德兹，
http://bejlt.brookes.ac.uk/article/architectural_psychology_19692007/。

39 http://www.defensiblespace.com/start.htm. 以及纽曼[1973]。应补充的一点是，被大量记录在案的与设计糟糕的社会住宅项目有关的的身体和心理疾病，通常主要是由经济和社会剥夺造成的，建筑的不良质量只是揭示了这个问题，又不可避免地使问题变得更加严重。

40 关于这个话题的深入讨论以及其他案例，参见[利奇，1999]。

41 只有当一个人从更广义的层面上去看待伦理学，这种方法才能够涵盖以上诸点；它需要在许多不同的要求之间达到总体的平衡，例如可持续性、效

ciency, positive psychological influences, or sensitivity to the stylistic context, as well as the demands of economy and society. This can *itself* be seen as an ethical task.

[42] Nevertheless, some would claim that architecture, in providing in some way a vision of a better life, can itself furnish ethical ideals – see [Harries, 1997].

[43] It is revealing that *Technology Assessment* is a relatively new term (coined in 1966) as much as a new science. And *Environmental Impact Assessment*, a formal process used to predict the environmental consequences of a development project, was not introduced as a planning and decision making tool before the late 1960s (in the United States in the *National Environmental Policy Act* of 1969).

[44] Values like "honesty" help at most in the first area; that is why professional ethics is the best developed sub-discipline of the built environment. We should also recall that the notion of the *polis* played a crucial role in Plato's ethics (see footnote 1 above).

[45] I.e., a proportion of $(a+b)/a = a/b = \phi$. For a discussion of proportion in architecture, see [Scholfield, 1958].

[46] The Golden Ratio also plays an important role in non-Western architecture, for example the Mosque from Kairouan (Tunisia) from 670 AD (see [Boussora and Mazouz, 2004]).

[47] Other rules or standards have been suggested by artists and philosophers such as William Hogarth in his *The Analysis of Beauty* (1753) or Joshua Reynolds in his *Seventh Discourse on Art* (1797). And Dalibor Vesely [2004] has argued that in the Baroque period ideas of proportion were derived from a world view, rather than being merely an instrumentalised process.

[48] Almost – Peter Eisenman, for example, does not think much of Chartres: "I think it is a boring building. [...] In fact, I have gone to Chartres a number of times to eat in the restaurant across the street – had a 1934 red Mersault wine, which was exquisite – I never went into the cathedral." (See the debate with Christopher Alexander, already referred to: http://www.katarxis3.com/Alexander_Eisenman_Debate.htm.)

[49] In brief the difficulties are as follows: how does one judge the differing opinions? Is the judgement of any lay person accepted – or do they have to be specially trained or knowledgeable or sensitive? It seems the "bottom-up approach" simply postpones the problem of whether a cognitivist or subjectivist account is more suitable to make an adequate judgement in the "trial".

[50] For a close reading of both the *Enquiry* and Burke's later book the *Reflections on the Revolution in France*, see [Furniss, 1993].

[51] An excellent general introduction to the picturesque is [Macarthur, 2007].

[52] For Goethe's important influence on Nineteenth Century aesthetic theory see [Mallgrave and Ikonomou, 1994].

[53] An idiosyncratic example is [Edwards, 2003], which sets out to examine "a chance remark by a friend that Aesthetics, traditionally an aspect of philosophy, is properly an aspect of psychology".

[54] It was titled *On the Optical Sense of Form: A Contribution to Aesthetics*. See [Mallgrave and Ikonomou, 1994].

[55] "Die Neue Welt", in *Das Werk 13*, 1926, in [Meyer, 1980], cited in [Kruft, 1994, p. 386].

[56] "Bauen", in *Bauhaus 2*, 1928, in [Meyer, 1980], cited in [Kruft, 1994, p. 386]. For the Bauhaus and its teaching see [Whitford, 1984].

[57] See [Carter, 1981]: "Schinkel lived during a period of transition, a period when the conventions of the Baroque could no longer be accepted and a variety of new tasks arising from the social and industrial revolutions demanded new solutions. The self-conscious attitude vis-à-vis the past promoted by archaeological investigation and historical speculation encouraged the notion of a new style appropriate to a new age, but the complexity of the new situation and the need for immediate action made a complete return to first principles impractical. While one waited for the new style to emerge, an eclectic approach could offer a temporary resolution [...] If similar forms could express such a variety of ideas, was it also possible that a variety of forms could express similar ideas? That meaning was not intrinsic in the forms but rather attached to them by tacit agreement and confirmed by the specific context?"

[58] For a discussion of proportional systems, which sometimes make this claim, see Scholfield 1958. The Finnish architect Alvar Aalto said his wooden furniture was more functional than the furniture designed

率、积极的心理影响，或对风格背景的敏感度，以及经济和社会层面的要求。这本身可以看作是一项伦理任务。

42 不过，一些人可能会说，建筑在某种意义上提供了一种关于更美好的生活的愿景，建筑本身能够提供伦理理念——见[哈里斯，1997]。

43 引人省思的是技术评估是一个相对较新的术语，如同一门新科学（形成于1966年）。环境影响评估，是预测某发展项目对环境造成的影响的一个正式流程，在二十世纪六十年代末（美国1969年发布了《国家环境政策法案》）之前还尚未成为一种规划和决策的手段。

44 "诚实"之类的价值观最多只在上文所列的第一个领域里有所帮助；这也是为什么职业伦理学是建筑环境发展最为成熟的二级学科。我们应该还记得，城邦的概念在柏拉图的伦理学中起着至关重要的作用（参见脚注42）。

45 即这样的一个比例：(a+b) ＝ a/b ＝ φ。有关建筑学中对比例的讨论，参见[斯科菲尔德（Scholfield），1958]。

46 黄金比例在非西方建筑中也发挥着重要作用，例如公元670年的凯鲁万清真寺（突尼斯）（参见 [波索拉和马佐兹（Boussora and Mazouz），2004]）。

47 有些艺术家和哲学家提出了其他的规则或标准，例如威廉·贺加斯（William Hogarth）《对美的分析》（1753）或是约书亚·雷诺兹（Joshua Reynolds）《关于艺术的第七篇论述》（1797）。达里波尔·维斯利（Dalibor Vesely）[2004]则认为，巴洛克时期关于比例的理念来自于某种世界观，而不仅仅是一个工具化的过程。

48 这里说的是"几乎"——例如彼得·艾森曼（Peter Eisenman）就不喜欢沙特尔大教堂："我认为它是一个无趣的建筑……实际上，我多次前往沙特尔大教堂，为的是在街对面的餐厅吃饭——来一杯 1934 年的默尔索红葡萄酒，一种非常高雅的酒——我从来没有进过大教堂。"（参见与克里斯托弗·亚历山大（Christopher Alexander）的辩论，已被提及：http://www.katarxis3.com/Alexander_Eisenman_Debate.htm.）

49 简单来讲，这些困难如下：一个人如何判断不同的意见？是否接受任何外行人的判断——或者该外行人是否必须受过专门培训或者知识渊博或者比较敏感？似乎"自下而上的方法"仅仅推迟了这样一个难题，即认知主义者还是主观主义者的理由更适合在"审判"中作出适当的判决。

50 欲详细阅读《探究》一书和伯克后来的作品《法国革命的思考》（Reflections on the Revolution in France）参见[弗尼斯（Furniss），1993 年]。

51 对风景美的很好的一般介绍见[麦克阿瑟（Macarthur），2007 年]。

52 关于哥德对十九世界美学理论的重要影响，参见[Mallgrave 和 Ikonomou，1994 年]。

53 一个特殊的例子是[Edwards，2003 年]，它打算探讨"一个朋友的偶然见解，即美学——传统上是哲学的一个分支——恰当地说是心理学的一个分支"。

54 其题目为《关于形式的视觉感知：对美学的一份贡献》（On the Optical Sense of Form: A Contribution to Aesthetics）。参见[Mallgrave 和 Ikonomou，1994 年]。

55 《新世界（Die Neue Welt）》，来自1926 年的 《工作集13》（Das Werk 13），又见[迈耶，1980 年]，引自[Knuft，1994 年，第 386 页]。

56 "建造（Bauen）"，在 1928 年的 《包豪斯2》中，又见[迈耶，1980 年]，引自[Kruft，1994 年，第 386 页]。关于包豪斯学院及其教学，参见[Whitford，1984 年]。

57 参见[卡特，1981 年]："席勒生活在一个过渡时期，这是巴洛克公约不再被接受并且社会和工业革命提出的各种新任务需要更新的解决方案的时期。与过去受考古调查和历史思辨推动的方式相比，自我觉醒的意识倡导适应新时代的新风格这一概念，但是新形势的复杂性和需要立即行动的迫切性，使得完全贯彻那些首要原则变得不切实际。当一个人在等待着新风格出现时，或许一个折中的方法便是提出一个暂时性的解决方案……如果相似的形式可以表达诸多不同的理念，那么诸多不同的形式是否也有可能表达相似的理念？意义并不是形式所固有的，而是通过人们默认的共识附加到形式之上的，再借由具体环境得以巩固？"

58 这种观点有时可见于关于比例系统的讨论之中，参见斯科菲尔德 1958。芬兰建筑师阿尔瓦·阿尔托表示，他的木制家具比同时代的

117

by his contemporaries in the Bauhaus, which was metal-framed, and cold to the touch. But he acknowledged that scientific analysis "gave out" at some point: "The demands that the chair failed to meet – excessive reflection of sound and light, high thermal conductivity – are actually merely the scientific names of the elements that together make up the mysterious concept of 'comfort'". ("Rationalismen och manniskän" Lecture at the annual meeting of the Swedish Society of Industrial Design, May 9 1935, reprinted in Schildt 1998)

[59] The example of Bentham's *Panopticon* is often quoted as an illustration of how building form can mesh closely with patterns of control. See, for example, Bauman 1992, pp. XVI-XVII. But precisely what form a "democratic architecture" would take is a complex question. See Wilson 1992.

[60] Panel discussion, 1960, reprinted in [Kahn, 1961], and [Kahn, 1991, pp. 112-120].

[61] Robert Venturi criticised Walter Gropius for perverting the Vitruvian trinity by suggesting that *utilitas* + *firmitas* = *venustas*, rather than seeing these three terms as equal participants in the definition of architecture. The teaching at the Bauhaus, where Gropius was Director from 1919 – 1927 was not as straightforwardly "functionalist" as has been often assumed (see [Rykwert, 1982]), but later, at the Harvard Graduate School of Design, where Gropius moved in 1937, the teaching programmes emphasised functional considerations as the only generators of architectural form (see [Herdeg, 1983]).

[62] Interview in *House and Garden*, October 1972, reprinted in [Kahn, 1991, p. 196].

[63] See, for example, the essay on Koolhaas in [Moneo, 2004].

[64] For the fullest account of Aalto's work and life see the three volume biography by Schildt [1984, 1986, 1989].

包豪斯一派设计的家具更具有功能性，后者为金属框架结构，摸起来冰凉——。但是他承认，科学分析在某种程度上也是"精疲力竭"："椅子未能达到的要求，例如对声音和光线的过度反射、高度导热性，实际上不过是一些科学称谓，所指的就是构成神秘的 '舒适'概念的那些组成元素。"（"Rationalismen och manniskän"，在瑞典工业设计协会年会上的讲话，1935 年 5 月 9 日，1998 年转载于 Schildt）

[59] 边沁（Bentham）的《圆形监狱》（Panopticon）经常被人们作为例子引用，来说明建筑形式如何能够高度符合监管模式。参见（例如）鲍曼（Bauman 1992），第16—17页。但"民主式建筑"要采用什么形式正是一个很复杂的问题。参见威尔逊（Wilson）1992。

[60] 小组讨论，1960，[康，1961]，[康，1991，第112-120页]再版。

[61] 罗伯特·文丘里批评瓦尔特·格罗皮乌斯滥用维特鲁威的建筑三要素，格罗皮乌斯提出实用（utilitas）+ 坚固（firmitas）=美（venustas），而不是将建筑定义中的这三个术语看做等同的三部分。格罗皮乌斯在1919年至1927年间担任包豪斯设计学院院长，该学院的教学并非如人们通常认为的那样是完全"功能主义的"（见[里克沃特，1982]），但随后，哈佛大学设计研究生院（格罗皮乌斯1937年搬到那里）的教学方案中则强调，功能方面的考量是建筑形式唯一促成因素（见[赫德格，1983]）。

[62] 《房屋和花园》中的采访，1972年10月，[康，1991，第196页]再版。

[63] 例如，参见库哈斯在[莫内欧，2004]的文章。

[64] 关于对阿尔托工作和生活的最完整的阐述，见希尔特所著的传记，共三卷[1984，1986，1989]。

Bibliography

参考文献

[Alberti, 1988] L. B. Alberti. *De re aedificatoria* 'On the art of building in ten books'. translated by Joseph Rykwert, Neil Leach, and Robert Tavernor. MIT Press, 1988.

[Alexander, 2002] C. Alexander. *The Phenomenon of Life* (vol. I of *The Nature of Order*). Center for Environmental Structure, Berkeley, 2002.

[van Armando, 1989] H. D. van D. Armando. Een internationale primeur. In *De nieuwe Stijl,* Sjoerd van Faassen and Hans Sleutelaar, eds. De Bezige Bij, 1989.

[Banham, 1966] R. Banham. *The New Brutalism: Ethic or Aesthetic?* Architectural Press, 1966.

[Batteux, 1746] C. Batteux, *Les beaux arts réduits à un même principe*, 1746.

[Baumgarten, 1961] A. G. Baumgarten. Aesthetica [Vol. 1 1750, Vol. 2 1758]. Olms, 1961.

[Benedikt, 1992] M. Benedikt. *Deconstructing the Kimbell: an Essay on Meaning and Architecture.* Lumen Inc., 1992.

[Bergilez and Genard, 2004] J. D. Bergilez and J. L. Genard. Minimalisme architectural: quand l'éthique s'inscrit dans le style. In *Intervalles 1: Minimalism(e)s.* Liège, CIPA, 2004. Retrieved October 20, 2007, from www.cipa.ulg.ac.be/ intervalles1/contents.htm.

[Buossora and Mazouz, 2004] K. Boussora and S. Mazouz. The Use of the Golden Section in the Great Mosque of Kairouan. In *Nexus Network Journal*, 6, 2004.

[Brawne, 1992] M. Brawne. *From Idea to Building.* Butterworth Heinemann Ltd, 1992.

[Burchardt, 1878] J. Burckhardt. *The Civilization of the Renaissance in Italy.* Translated by S. G. C. Middlemore, 1878. Republished by Penguin, 1990.

[Burke, 1990] E. Burke. *A Philosophical Enquiry Into the Origin of Our Ideas of the Sublime and the Beautiful* [1759]. ed. Adam Phillips. Oxford University Press, 1990.

[Carter, 1981] R. Carter. Karl Friedrich Schinkel: The last Great Architect. In *Collection of Architectural Designs including those designs which have been executed and objects whose execution was intended by Karl Friedrich Schinkel*, Carter, Rand, ed. Exedra Books Incorporated, 1981. Retreived September 5, 2008.

[Coleman, 1990] A. M. Coleman. *Utopia on Trial: Vision and Reality in Planned Housing.* Hilary Shipman Ltd, 1990.

[Collins, 1971] P. Collins. *Architectural Judgement.* University of Toronto Press, 1971.

[Colquhoun, 1985] A. Colquhoun. *Essays in Architectural Criticism.* MIT Press, 1985.

[Curtis, 1982] W. Curtis. *Modern Architecture Since 1900.* Phaidon Press, 1982.

[Curtis, 1986] W. Curtis. *Le Corbusier: Ideas and Forms.* Phaidon Press, 1986.

[Davies, 1994] S. Davies. Is Architecture Art?. In *Philosophy and Architecture.* M. H. Mitias, ed., pp. 31-47. Rodopi, 1994.

[Dewey, 1988] J. Dewey. Human Nature and Conduct. In *The Collected Works of John Dewey (Middle Works Vol. 14)*, Boydston, Jo Ann, ed., pp. 21-32. Southern Illinois University Press, 1988.

[Dutch Royal Society of Architects, 2007] Dutch Royal Society of Architects. *Gedragsregels van de Koninklijke Maatschappij tot Bevordering der Bouwkunst Bond van Nederlandse Architecten.* 1998. Retrieved August 25, 2007, from http://www.bna.nl.

[Eardely, 1973] A. Eardley, (trans.) *The Charter of Athens.* Grossman, 1973.

[Edwards, 2003] A. Edwards. *Images of Eden, an enquiry into the psychology of architecture.* The Skylark Press, 2003.

[Eliade, 1971] M. Eliade. *The Myth of the Eternal Return.* Bollingen, 1971.

[Fisher, 2000] S. Fisher. How to think about the ethics of architecture. In *Ethics and the built environment*, Fox, W., ed., pp. 170-182. Routledge, 2000.

[Forty, 2000] A. Forty. *Words and Buildings: A Vocabulary of Modern Architecture.* Thames and Hudson, 2000.

[Fox, 2000] W. Fox, ed. *Ethics and the Built Environment.* Routledge, 2000.

[Fox, 2007] W. Fox. *A Theory of General Ethics, Human Relationships, Nature and the Built Environment.* MIT Press, 2007.

[Fox, 2008] W. Fox. Architecture ethics. In *A Companion to Philosophy of Technology*, Berg, J.-K. and Hendricks, V. F., eds. Blackwell, 2008.

[Frampton, 1980] K. Frampton. *Modern Architecture, a Critical History.* Thames and Hudson, 1980.

[Frampton, 1983] K. Frampton. Towards a Critical Regionalism: Six Points for an Architecture of Resistance. In *The Anti-Aesthetic*, Foster, Hal, ed. Bay Press, 1983.

[Furniss, 1993] T. Furniss. *Edmund Burke's Aesthetic Ideology.* Cambridge University Press, 1993.

[Gadamer, 1983] H.-G. Gadamer. What is Practice? In *Reason in the Age of Science* [Vernunft im

Zeitalter der Wissenschaft, 1976]. MIT Press, 1983.
[Gadamer, 1989] H.-G. Gadamer. *Truth and Method* [Wahrheit und Methode, 1960]. 2nd revised edition. trans. J. Weinsheimer and D.G.Marshall. Crossroad, 1989.

[Gauldie, 1969] W. S. Gauldie. *Architecture (Appreciation of Arts)*. Oxford University Press, 1969.

[Games, 1985] S. Games. *Behind the Fa.cade*. BBC Arial Books, 1985.

[Giedion, 1962] S. Giedion. *Space, Time and Architecture*. The Charles Eliot Norton Lectures 1938-9. Oxford University Press, 1962.

[Gilpin, 1792] W. Gilpin. *Three Essays: On Picturesque Beauty; on Picturesque travel; and On Sketching Landscape*. London, 1792.

[Gombrich, 1979] E. Gombrich. *The Story of Art*. Phaidon, 1979.

[Goodman 1976]. N. Goodman. *Languages of Art*. Hackett Publishing Company.1976.

[Guy and Farmer, 2000] S. Guy and G. Farmer. Contested constructions. The competing logics of green buildings and ethics. In *Ethics and the Built Environment*, Fox, Warwick, ed., pp. 73-87. Routledge, 2000.

[Harries, 1975] K. Harries. The ethical function of architecture. In *Journal of Architectural Education*, 29/1, pp. 14-15, 1975.

[Harries, 1997] K. Harries. *The ethical function of architecture*, MIT Press, 1997.

[Heidegger, 1977] M. Heidegger. The Age of the World Picture [Die Zeit des Weltbildes, 1938]. In *The Question concerning Technology and Other Essays*. trans. W. Lovett. Harper and Row, 1977.

[Heidegger, 1993] M. Heidegger. Building, Dwelling, Thinking [Bauen, Wohnen, Denken, 1951]. In *Basic Writings*, Krell, David Farrell, ed., pp. 347-363. Routledge, 1993.

[Heisenberg, 1958] W. Heisenberg. *The Physicist's Conception of Nature*. Hutchinson, 1958.

[Herdeg, 1983] K. Herdeg. *The Decorated Diagram: Harvard Architecture and the failure of the Bauhaus Legacy*. MIT Press, 1983.

[Herodotus, 1987] Herodotus. *The History*. University of Chicago Press, 1987.

[Hillier, 1986] B. Hillier. City of Alice's Dreams. *Architect's Journal*, Vol. 39-41, 1986.

[Hillier and Iida, 2005] B. Hillier and S. Iida. Network and psychological effects in urban movement. In *Proceedings of Spatial Information Theory: International Conference, COSIT*, Cohn, A.G. and Mark, D.M., eds., pp. 475-490. Springer, 2005.

[Hume, 1965] D. Hume. *Of the Standard of Taste* [1757] and *Other Essays*. The Library of Liberal Arts, 1965.

[Husserl, 1970] E. Husserl. *The Crisis of European Sciences and Transcendental Phenomenology*. Northwestern University Press, 1970.

[Ihde, 2008] D. Ihde. The Designer Fallacy and Technological Imagination, In *Philosophy and Design: From Engineering to Architecture*, Kroes, P. and Vermaas, P.E. and Light, A. and Moore, S. A., eds., pp. 51-59. Springer, 2008.

[Illies, 2005] C. Illies. Architektur als Kunst. *Zeitschrift für Ästhetik und Allgemeine Kunstwissenschaft*, 50/1, pp. 57-76, 2005.

[Illies, 2008] C. Illies. The moral relevance of architecture. *IAPS Bulletin*, 31, pp. 3-6, 2008.

[Jencks, 1975] C. Jencks. *Le Corbusier and the Tragic View of Architecture*. Allen Lane, 1975.

[Kahn, 1961] L. I. Kahn. Form and Design. *Architectural Design* XXXI, 4, pp. 130-149, 1961.

[Kahn, 1991] L. I. Kahn. *Writings, Lectures, Interviews*. Rizzoli, 1991.

[Kant, 1962] I. Kant. *Critique of Judgement* [Kritik der Urteilskraft, 1790]. transl. James Creed Meredith. Clarendon Press, 1962.

[Koolhaas and Mau, 1995] R. Koolhaas B. Mau. *S, M, L, XL*. Jennifer Sigler, ed. 010 Publishers, 1995.

[Kris, 1953] E. Kris. *Psychoanalytic Explorations in Art*. Allen & Unwin, 1953.

[Kroes and Primus, 2008 P. Kroes and H. Primus. Technical artefacts as physical and social constructions: the case of Cité de la Muette. *Housing Studies*, 23:5, pp. 717-736, 2008.

[Kruft, 1994] H.-W. Kruft. *A History of Architectural Theory from Vitruvius to the Present*. Princeton Architectural Press, 1994.

[Le Corbusier, 1946] Le Corbusier. *Towards a New Architecture*. Transl. Frederick Etchells. The Architectural Press, 1946. (originally published as *Vers Une Architecture*. Éditions Crès, 1923.)

[Leach, 1997] N. Leach, ed. *Rethinking Architecture: a reader in cultural theory*. Routledge, 1997.

[Leach, 1999] N. Leach. *Architecture and Revolution:Contemporary Perspectives on Central and Eastern Europe*. Routledge, 1999.

[Leach, 2002] N. Leach. Forget Heidegger. In *Designing for a Digital World*, Leach, Neil, ed., pp. 21-30. Wiley, 2002.

[Lethaby, 1955] W. Lethaby. *Architecture: An Introduction to the History and Theory of the Art of Building*. Oxford University Press, 1955.

[Lipman, 2003] A. Lipman. *Architecture on My Mind: Critical Readings in Design*. Unisa Press, 2003.

[Loran 2007] R. Lorand. In Defense of Beauty. *Aesthetics on line* 2007. Retrived 2014-04-18 http://www.aesthetics-online.org/articles/index.php?articles_id=34

[Lovejoy, 1927] A. O. Lovejoy. 'Nature' as Aesthetic Norm. *Modern Language Notes*, 42/7, pp. 444-450, 1927.

[Macarthur, 2007] J. Macarthur. *The Picturesque: Architecture, disgust, and other irregularities*. London and New York, Routledge, 2007.

[Mallgrave, 1994] H. F. Mallgrave and E. Ikonomou, eds. *Empathy, Form and Space, Problems in German Aesthetics 1873-1893*. Getty Center for the History of Art and the Humanities, 1994.

[Mandelbaum, 1967] M. Mandelbaum. Historicism. In *Encyclopedia of Philosophy*. Macmillan and The Free Press, 1967.

[Massey, 1994] D. Massey. *Space, place, and gender*. University of Minnesota Press, 1994.

[McCarter, 2005] R. McCarter. *Louis Kahn*. Phaidon Press, 2005.

[Meagher, 2008] S. M. Meagher. *Philosophy and the City: Classic to Contemporary Writings*. State University of New York Press, 2008.

[Meinecke, 1946] F. Meinecke. *Die Entstehung des Historismus*. Leibniz Verlag, 1946.

[Meyer, 1980] H. Meyer. *Bauen und Gesellschaft. Schriften, Briefe, Projekte*. Verlag der Kunst, 1980.

[Mikellides, 2008] B. Mikellides. Architectural Psychology 1969-2003, Theory, Practise and Education. *Brookes Journal of Learning and Teaching*, Vol. 2, Issue 2, 2007. Retrieved September 5 2008 from http://bejlt.brookes.ac.uk/article/architectural_psychology_19692007.

[Modiano, 1994] R. Modiano. The legacy of the Picturesque. In *The Politics of the Picturesque*, Copley, S. and Garside, P., eds. Cambridge University Press, 1994.

[Moneo, 2004] R. Moneo. *Theoretical Anxiety and Design Strategies*. MIT Press, 2004.

[Moneo 2004] R. Moneo. Lecture to 'Anwhere' conference, Yufuin, Japan, 1992, re-printed pp. 635-641 in *20+64+98 Rafael Moneo 1967-2004*, El Croquis Editorial 2004

[Moore, 1966] H. Moore. The sculptor speaks. In *Henry Moore on Sculpture*, James, Philip, ed., pp. 62-64. MacDonald, 1966.

[Moritz, 1788] K. P. Moritz. *Über die bildende Nachahmung des Schönen*. Braunschweig, 1788.

[Mostafavi and Leatherbarrow, 1993] M. Mostafavi and D Leatherbarrow, *On Weathering: the Life of Buildings in Time*, MIT, 1993.

[Muschamp, 2000] H. Muschamp. *New York Times*, 18th June 2000.

[Nagel, 1979] T. Nagel. *Mortal Questions*. Cambridge University Press, 1979.

[Neumeyer 1989]. F. Neumeyer. *Quellentexte zur Architekturtheorie. Bauen beim Wort genommen*, Prestel 1989 (2002).

[Newman, 1973] O. Newman. *Defensible Space: Crime Prevention through Urban Design*. Macmillan, 1973.

[Nietzsche, 2000] F. Nietzsche. *The Birth of Tragedy from the Spirit of Music* [Die Geburt der Tragödie aus dem Geiste der Musik, 1872]. Oxford University Press, 2000.

[Norberg-Schulz, 1966] C. Norberg-Schulz. *Intentions in Architecture*. MIT Press, 1966.

[Norberg-Schulz, 1971] C. Norberg-Schulz. *Existence, Space and Architecture*. Praeger, 1971.

[Norberg-Schulz, 1990] C. Norberg-Schulz. *Genius Loci: Towards a Phenomenology of Architecture*, Rizzoli, 1990.

[Osmond, 1957] H. Osmond. Function as the Basis of Psychiatric Ward Design, *Mental Hospitals*, 8, pp. 23-29, 1957.

[Pallasmaa, 2005] J. Pallasmaa. *Touching the World – Architecture, Hapticity, and the Emancipation of the Eye*, speech on the honorary PhD at the University of Helsinki, retrieved on: www.enhsa.net/downloads/2005proceedings/ 06pallasmaa.pdf

[Panofsky, 1957] E. Panofsky. *Gothic Architecture and Scholasticism*. Meridian Books, 1957.

[Panofsky, 1968] E. Panofsky. *Idea, a concept in art theory*. University of South Carolina Press, 1968.

[Passmore 1954] J. A. Passmore, The Dreariness of Aesthetics. In *Aesthetics and Language*, Elton, W. ed., pp. 36-55. Blackwell, 1954,.

[Pepper, 1984] D. Pepper. *The Roots of Modern Environmentalism*. Routledge, 1984.

[Pevsner, 1943] N. Pevsner. *An Outline of European Architecture*. Penguin, 1943.

[Plato, 1945] Plato. *Republic*. Trans. F. M. Cornford. Oxford University Press, 1945.

[Popper, 1959] K. Popper. *The Logic of Scientific Discovery*. Basic Books, 1959.

[Posener, 1978] J. Posener. Eine Architektur für das Glück? In *Was ist Glück?*, Carl Friedrich von Siemens Stiftung, ed., pp. 149-170. Deutscher Taschenbuchverlag, 1978.

[Price, 1842] U. Price. An Essay on the Picturesque, as compared with the Sublime and the Beautiful. In *Sir Uvedale Price on the Picturesque*. Lauder, Dick, ed. Edinburgh, 1842.

[Pugin, 1843] A. W. N. Pugin. *An Apology for the Revival of Christian Architecture in England*. John Weale, 1843.

[Punter, 1994] D. Punter. The Picturesque and the Sublime: two worldscapes. In *The Politics of the Picturesque*, Copley, S. and Garside, P., eds., Cambridge University Press, 1994.

[Pye 2002] D. Pye. *The Nature and Aesthetics of Design*, Berg 3PL, 2002

[Ramroth, 2006] W. G. Ramroth. *Pragmatism and Modern Architecture*. McFarland, 2006.

[Rapoport, 1969] A. Rapoport. *House Form and Culture*. Prentice-Hall, 1969.

[Rapoport, 1990] A. Rapoport. *The Meaning of the Built Environment: A Non-Verbal Communication Approach*. University of Arizona Press, 1990.

[Ray, 2005a] N. Ray. *Alvar Aalto*. Yale University Press, 2005.

[Ray, 2005b] N. Ray, ed. *Architecture and its Ethical Dilemmas*. Taylor & Francis, 2005.

[Roberts, 2005] J. Roberts. Architecture, Morality and Taste. In *Architecture and its Ethical Dilemmas*, Ray, Nicholas, ed. Taylor & Francis, 2005.

[Rowe and Koetter, 1978] C. Rowe and F. Koetter. *Collage City*. MIT Press, 1978.

[Ruskin, 1878-79] J. Ruskin. *Modern Painters* (5 Vol.). John Wiley, 1878-79.

[Rykwert, 1982] J. Rykwert. The Dark Side of the Bauhaus. In *The Necessity of Artifice*. Rizzoli, 1982.

[Rzchtarikova and Akkerman, 2003] J. Rzchtarikova and A. Akkerman. Trajectories of fertility and household composition in the demographic profile of the Czech Republic. *Population and Environment*, 24 (3), pp. 225-254, 2003.

[Scott, 1980] G. Scott. *The Architecture of Humanism*. Architectural Press, 1980.

[Schiller, 1983] F. Schiller. *Letters upon the AEsthetic Education of Man* [Über die ästhetische Erziehung des Menschen, 1795]. Clarendon Press, 1983.

[Schildt, 1984-89] G. Schildt. *Alvar Aalto: the Early Years; the Decisive Years, the Mature Years*. Rizzoli, 1984, 1986, 1989.

[Schildt, 1998] G. Schildt, ed. *Alvar Aalto in his own words*. Rizzoli International, 1998.

[Scholfield, 1958] P. H. Scholfield. *The Theory of Proportion in Architecture*. Cambridge University Press, 1958.

[Schön, 1983] D. A. Schön. *The Reflective Practitioner: How Professionals think in action*. Basic Books, 1983.

[Schopenhauer, 1849] A. Schopenhauer. *Die Welt als Wille und Vorstellung*. [1859] Berlin und Wien, 1924.

[Scruton, 1979] R. Scruton. *The Aesthetics of Architecture*. Princeton University Press, 1979.

[Scruton, 2000] R. Scruton. After Modernism. *City Journal*, Spring 2000.

[Simon, 1969] H. A. Simon. *The Sciences of the Artificial*. MIT Press, 1969.

[Spector, 2001] T. Spector. *The Ethical Architect: The Dilemma of Contemporary Practice*. Princeton Architectural Press, 2001.

[Spector, 2004] T. Spector. Pragmatism for Architects. *Contemporary Pragmatism*, Vol. 1/1, pp. 133-149, 2004.

[Spector, 2005] T. Spector. Codes of Ethics and Coercion. In Ray, Nicolas, ed., *Architecture and its Ethical Dilemmas*, Taylor & Francis, 2005.

[Stokes, 2002] A. Stokes. *The Quattro Cento and The Stones of Rimini*. First combined edition, Ashgate Publishers Ld, Aldershot, 2002.

[Sullivan, 1886] L. Sullivan. Essay on Inspiration. *Inland Architect*, 8:2, pp. 61-64, 1886.

[Sullivan, 1924] L. Sullivan. *Autobiography of an Idea*. Pess of the American Institute of Architects, Inc, New York City, 1924. Republished by Reprint Services Corp, 1991.

[Summerson, 1966] J. Summerson. *The Classical Language of Architecture*. MIT Press, 1966.

[Taylor, 1991] C. Taylor. *The Malaise of Modernity*. Anansi, 1991.

[Taylor and Levine 2011] W. Taylor and M. Levine, *Prospects for an ethics of Architecture*, Routledge, 2011

[Tillich, 1952] P. Tillich. Being and Love. In *Moral Principles in Action*, Anshen, R. N, ed., pp. 661-672. Harper, 1952.

[*Time* 1938]. Usonian Architech. *TIME magazine* Jan. 17, 1938. 1938-01-17. Retrieved 2014-04-14.

[Van Eyck, 1999] A. Van Eyck. *Works 1944-99*. Birkhouser Verlag AG, 1999.

[van Leeuwen, Macrae, 2004] M. L. van Leeuwen and C. N. Macrae. Is Beautiful Always Good? Implicit Benefits of Facial Attractiveness. *Social Cognition*: Vol. 22, No. 6, pp. 637-649, 2004.

[Venturi, 2006] R. Venturi. *Complexity and Contradiction in Architecture*. New York, Museum of Modern Art, 2006.

[Venturi and Scott-Brown, 1972] R. Venturi and D. Scott-Brown. *Learning from Las Vegas*. MIT Press, 1972.

[Vesely, 2004] D. Vesely. *Architecture in the Age of Divided Representation*. MIT Press, 2004.

[Vischer, 1994] R. Vischer. On the Optical Sense of Form: a Contribution to Aesthetics. In *Empathy, Form, and Space: Problems in German Aesthetics, 1873-1893*, Getty Center for the History of Art and the Humanities, ed. University of Chicago Press, 1994.

[Vitruvius, 2001] Vitruvius. *Ten Books on Architecture*. ed. Ingrid D Rowland. Cambridge University Press, 2001.

[Wasserman et al., 2000] B. Wasserman, P. J. Sullivan, and G. Palermo. *Ethics and the Practice of Architecture*. John Wiley, 2000.

[Watkin, 1977] D. Watkin. *Morality and Architecture: the development of a theme in architectural history and theory from the Gothic Revival to the Modern Movement*. Clarendon Press, 1977.

[Welsch, 1996] W. Welsch. *Grenzgänge der Ästhetik*. Reclam, 1996.

[Whitford, 1984] F. Whitford. *Bauhaus*. Thames and Hudson, 1984.

[Wigley, 1992] M. Wigley. Heidegger's House: the violence of the domestic. In *Columbia Documents of Architecture and Theory*, D 1, 1992.

[Wilde, 1990] O. Wilde. The Picture of Dorian Gray. In *The Complete Works of Oscar Wilde*, pp. 17-167. Enderby, 1990.

[Williams, 1981] B. Williams. *Moral Luck, philosophical papers 1973-1980*. Cambridge University Press, 1981.

[Williamson and Radford, 2000] T. Williamson and A. Radford. Building, Global Warming and Ethics. In *Ethics and the Built Environment*. Fox, Warwick, ed., pp. 57-73. Routledge, 2000.

[Wimsatt, 1954] W. K. Wimsatt, Jr. and M. C. Beardsley. The intentional fallacy. In *The Verbal Icon: Studies in the Meaning of Poetry*. University of Kentucky Press, 1954.

[Wittgenstein, 1980] L. Wittgenstein. *Culture and Value* [Vermischte Bemerkungen, 1977]. ed. G.H. von Wright and Heikki Nyman, trans. Peter Winch. Blackwell, 1980.

[Wittkower, 1949] R. Wittkower. *Architectural Principles in the Age of Humanism*. The Warburg Institute, University of London, 1949.

[Woessner, 2003] M. Woessner. Ethics, architecture and Heidegger. 'Building Dwelling Thinking' in an American context. *City*, Vol.7/1, pp. 22-44, 2003.

[Wölfflin, 1886] H. Wölfflin. *Prolegomena to a Psychology of Architecture*, PhD Thesis, University of Munich, 1886.

[Wölfflin, 1950] H. Wölfflin. *Principles of Art History, The Problem of the Development of Style in Later Art*. trans. M. Hottinger. Dover Publications, 1950.

[Wright 1954] F. Lloyd Wright. *The Natural House* (New York: Bramhall House),1954

[Young, 2002] J. Young. *Heidegger's Later Philosophy*. Cambridge University Press, 2002.

Printed and bound by CPI Group (UK) Ltd, Croydon, CR0 4YY

13/04/2025

14656573-0001